Please do not write in this book

Please use scrap paper for any exercises

Unleashing Leaders

Unleashing Leaders

Developing Organizations for Leaders

Hilarie Owen

JOHN WILEY & SONS, LTD

Chichester • New York • Weinheim • Brisbane • Singapore • Toronto

Other Wiley Editorial Offices

John Wiley & Sons, Inc., 605 Third Avenue,
New York, NY 10158-0012, USA

WILEY-VCH Verlag GmbH, Pappelallee 3,
D-69469 Weinheim, Germany

John Wiley & Sons Australia Ltd, 33 Park Road, Milton,
Queensland 4064, Australia

John Wiley & Sons (Asia) Pte Ltd, 2 Clementi Loop #02-01,
Jin Xing Distripark, Singapore 129809

John Wiley & Sons (Canada) Ltd, 22 Worcester Road,
Rexdale, Ontario M9W 1L1, Canada

British Library Cataloguing in Publication Data

A catalogue record for this book is available from the British Library

ISBN 0-471-49613-8

Typeset in 11/15pt Goudy by Mayhew Typesetting, Rhayader, Powys
Printed and bound in Great Britain by Biddles Ltd, Guildford and King's Lynn
This book is printed on acid-free paper responsibly manufactured from sustainable forestry, in which
at least two trees are planted for each one used for paper production.

Contents

Preface vii

Acknowledgements xi

Introduction xiii

Are we ready for unleashing leaders?

1: How We Develop Leaders Today 1

Are we doing it right?

2: The Problems of Organizational Life Today 11

Transformation and leadership are the challenges for everyone

3: The Good, the Bad and the Ugly 29

What we are seeing in organizations today is not leadership

4: The Time Traveller 65

The lessons for organizations from ancient times

5: Shaping Modern Organizations 85

Why do we build hierarchical structures ruled by managers?

6: The Paradigm for Change 93

A universal framework for leaders in the twenty-first century

7: Building a New Model for Organizations 113

To unleash leaders we make the old model obsolete

8:   Unleashing Leaders   135

Transforming individuals and organizations together

Conclusion: From Homo Sapiens to Homo Proteus
(Shape Changer Being)   149

We are all part of the journey – unleashing leaders is one step

References   155

Index   163

Preface

Every single thing is somehow the expression and incarnation of a thought. If a thing had never been a thought, it could never be.

David Bohm

For the last ten years I have been involved in developing and running leadership programmes for individuals. From this experience it became clear that even the best training programme is insufficient to enable someone to express their leadership fully and be a leader when the organization they work in hasn't also developed, learned and transformed. The converse is also true. In addition the changes in organizations we have seen over the last 20 years may have felt difficult but have been limited in their outcomes because of the structures and thinking that remain. These thoughts led to the conclusion that both organization and individuals have to develop together – but in both cases the change has to be more than we have seen in the last decade.

The result of all this is two books. The first, *In Search of Leaders*, came out in May 2000 and focused on the individual and how they could develop the very essence of leadership. The heart of the book is based on the belief that leadership is not about position in a hierarchy nor is it dependent on whether people report to individuals. Real leadership is a gift in every human being – be that gift small or large. It is part of being human and is expressed differently in every individual.

There never has been anyone who expressed their own leadership in the same way as another person. Just as every person is unique, with a unique DNA profile, so too is their leadership. This is fundamental to those training leaders or developing competency models in leadership for both are problematic.

What is vital is that people find out who they are and express this in their leadership. This doesn't necessarily require training in its present form. There is a need for greater understanding of leadership and clarification of the difference between management and leadership. *In Search of Leaders* tried to address this and in doing so takes the reader on an odyssey to find out who they are and who they can be as a leader. There is no right way or 'style' for being a leader but there is a richness in the expression of leadership. The problem is that most people are not aware of their leadership potential, and organizations in their present state do not encourage them to find it or use it.

This is why the second book was necessary. *Unleashing Leaders* tackles the whole issue of developing organizations so that individuals can be leaders everywhere within them. During the last 20 years organizations have seen change that has put strain and stress on individuals. However, real transformation has been elusive mainly because it was not desired. Today there is a growing realization that we are on the edge of a huge world paradigm shift and organizational transformation will be part of this. As we struggle to get to grips with new technology, globalization and a world of chaos the realization becomes more acute. What has been missing so far is, first, an insight into this new future and, second, the steps to take us there. It is only when this occurs that leadership will be unleashed throughout organizations. This book is an attempt to offer these two missing elements. Together the two books form the basis of developing leaders and organizations in the twenty-first century.

One final point. These are just one person's contribution and as such do not resolve all the issues. The hope is that they will encourage discussion, debate and dialogue and at least challenge some of our thinking. For as Einstein said, 'The problems we face cannot be resolved at the same level of thinking as that which gave rise to them.'

In other words we have to challenge our present thinking and be brave enough to do things in a different way. Many individuals are not doing this in both our public and private sector organizations so the outcome is to try and resolve issues the same way as has been tried over and over again whether the setting is another government initiative or another downsizing.

Unleashing Leaders is an attempt to approach and resolve the issue of enabling everyone to be leaders by sometimes thinking the unthinkable and saying what others think but do not say. For this reason I know some of the comments and ideas here will be uncomfortable for many. If this book makes you ask questions about yourself, your organization, your work or how you think, then the hours of writing it will have been worthwhile.

Therefore may I repeat the words physicist Neils Bohr used to say before his lectures when he was trying to explain a new phenomenon in quantum physics: 'Every sentence that I utter should not be considered as an assurance but as a question.'

Acknowledgements

No one knows the hard work, research, discipline and soul searching that goes into writing a book unless they have tried it. Thank goodness for friends who listen and encourage. Therefore I would like to thank Ruth, Cheryl, Liz, Anne, Barbara and Ivan; each of whom have listened to my ideas and encouraged me to be brave and express them in this book – even though at times they have commented, 'Are you sure you come from this planet? Where do you get this knowledge and understanding from?'

I've often wondered where the creative ideas come from and guess my parents must have had something to do with this. As a small child my mother drilled into me two things. The first was that the most important thing in life was education and learning. That yearning for knowledge has never dwindled. The second was determination. She would say: 'There's no such word as "Can't", Hilarie. If you really want to do something you will find a way.' My father, on the other hand gave me two very different gifts. The first was the most amazing love and from this he taught me that giving and loving made a person far richer than money. The second lesson my father taught me was to go out into the world and explore, try new things and see the world with amazement and enthusiasm. Thank you, Mum and Dad, for your gifts.

However, a book would not be published without a publisher and editor. Therefore I would like to thank Claire Plimmer and the rest of the team at John Wiley who have all contributed to the finished product.

Finally, thank you to my son Darren. Every day I wonder at you and feel so proud. Thank you Mavis and Dick for always being there.

I dedicate this book to my sister Avril who works every day to develop imagination, creativity and knowledge in her pupils.

Introduction

If humanity is entering a new world and a new consciousness, if a transformative shift is truly going on, then we must be awake to it and be part of it.

David Spangler

*T*here is absolutely no doubt in my mind that we *are* entering a new world and a new consciousness. This new world is much more than a technological advance – it will be new in respect of our thinking, way of seeing the world, spirituality, values and working life. The question is: are we *all* going to be awake to it and be part of it?

Many organizations are talking about unleashing leadership throughout, but is this what they *really* want? Do directors and senior managers want leadership throughout their organizations? Many do not, for they see it as threatening their very power base. Yet resistance will be futile because transformation is coming and – like a tidal wave – will be unstoppable.

Management is not working – particularly in the UK where resistance to change is strong and where downsizing or restructuring has been more difficult to accomplish than in most other countries. We have tried everything – from total quality, benchmarking and business process re-engineering to downsizing and restructuring. At the present time everyone is talking about leadership. Is this yet another attempt to 'fix things'? The danger is that we treat it as such. If we try to develop leadership as we have developed management, we will fail.

Many organizations use psychometric tests and training programmes to argue that they are developing people. The truth is the tests tell us little and many individuals on training programmes end up playing a 'role'. When the individuals return to work very little changes and working life goes on with more targets to achieve and longer hours to put in to achieve them.

Does it have to be like this? New 'ideas' come along such as competency frameworks; mind, body, spirit approaches or theatre activities. New training programmes are developed under the banner of 'leadership'. Does this produce the required leadership in organizations?

Unleashing Leaders tries to answer these questions and issues. It begins with a snapshot of what is happening in organizations in the USA and UK in the area of developing leaders. The next stage of the book takes a deeper look at the reality in organizations today. The picture is not particularly good but it is changing. For the last decade organizations have been travelling through a dark tunnel that has been frightening at times for many passengers. Some have jumped off. Now a glimmer of light is showing for a handful of organizations – but more need to see the lights.

To help the lights appear the next part of the book takes an unusual journey – back into the far distant past where we see the foundations and beginnings of organizations. There are lessons in everything we do including our history. Returning to the present we discover the answer to why we keep doing the same over and over again, and that this pattern needs to be addressed in order to evolve to the next stage.

The strains and difficulties of the last 20 years exemplify the tension of leaving a past world behind and entering a new one. Unleashing Leaders shows us a framework for the future – a framework to help us shift to a new transformative state in the twenty-first century. Already individuals are aware of the new consciousness emerging but the power of the past is holding most back. To move forward many will have to leave behind things once fought for in the corporate world: position, power, control and status.

Finally, the book takes the reader through a step-by-step process on the journey to the end of the tunnel. These steps involve learning and transformation for both individuals and organization. For the time is right for unleashing leaders throughout organizations. As Shakespeare wrote:

There is a tide in the affairs of men,
Which, taken at the flood, leads on to fortune;
Omitted, all the voyage of their life
Is bound in shallows and in miseries.
On such a full sea are we now afloat,
And we must take the current when it serves,
Or lose our ventures.
                                                Julius Caesar

The tide is high and we should all participate. *Unleashing Leaders* captures the way for *all* to participate in the transformation.

1

How We Develop Leaders Today

What we need is a radical change in our perspective of what it takes to truly create new generations of leaders.

Jay Conger

*D*uring the last five years many organizations have realized that management isn't good enough and that they do not have the necessary leadership capability throughout to achieve the best in a fast-changing, global world. 'Leadership at all levels of an organization is fundamental to the success of an enterprise.'[1] This recognition has prompted a range of activities to develop leadership and it is this that we will now focus on.

Throughout the UK, the rest of Europe and the USA the focus of the activities has been on training and development programmes that have included activities and guest speakers. This has been offered to managers or fast-track executives. In addition, some organizations have paid large sums of money on university courses including MBAs. For those who realize that developing leadership is ongoing, the activities have also included 360-degree feedback, executive coaching programmes and encouraging people to use the internal library for books and videos on leadership.

Is this effective? Research in the USA found that the least effective were the university programmes.[2] As for training courses the impact varied. The question we need to ask is whether a five-day programme could change the thinking and mindset of those attending? Many managers arrive on programmes believing that after learning a set of techniques and skills, they will return to work as leaders. This idea is often propagated by the courses on offer. Therefore, one of the first things is a need to get the message across that attending a leadership programme will not change managers into leaders – but it is a starting point. Leadership is an ongoing process of learning about oneself and the world.

Throughout the world, many training programmes explain leadership as a set of skills or techniques that can be learned. They also give the impression that leadership can be added or bolted on to management. This belief enables training organizations to provide their 'normal' training programmes. However, this is a serious weakness in developing leaders. Learning techniques may allow an individual to become a better manager but leadership is more about taking an inward journey and finding your own strengths and leadership gifts. In addition, management and leadership require different thinking and world views and therefore cannot be bolted together.

However, the biggest stumbling block is that on returning to the workplace, delegates are back in cultures and structures that prevent them from expressing and practising their leadership. This is particularly a problem when the values of the organization are in conflict with the values needed for leadership throughout or when the day-to-day demands are put above the development of individuals.

An example of this followed a six-month leadership programme I ran with a company. The delegates were senior managers who had been identified as having board potential. The programme was hugely successful in that it enabled the delegates to explore their own potential and express their leadership confidently in the workplace. The programme was reinforced with a company project, for which the delegates were responsible, set up by the managing director. However, on returning to work the managing director told them that the company was too busy and the project never happened. The delegates found this terribly disheartening and the message they took from this was, 'We don't have time for ongoing development and it certainly isn't a priority here.'

Training Leaders

How do different organizations develop leaders? Here is a summary of what is happening at present. An example in the UK is a company in the financial services sector. 'Leadership' was a word used by the executives who wrote their business strategy. Their first approach to developing leaders was to run a 'fast-track' programme for those identified as having 'potential'. Included in this programme was leadership. The whole programme itself was good but the culture of the company required task-oriented individuals whose performance was judged on targets and results. It didn't matter how they achieved as long as the targets were achieved. This meant that all learning was judged according to how much it could help them achieve their targets. Personal growth and development was in reality compliance.

The company had training centres in France and the USA where managing change was taught. It was a global company with global values that included team spirit. However, the reality fell short. Individuals were concerned about redundancies and whether they could achieve their targets. This made conditions very difficult for teamwork.

One of the biggest problems in the company was the presence of 'older' managers who had succeeded by behaving in a certain way that had been rewarded. These individuals were now being told that the world had changed and that a different behaviour was required. Following mergers and acquisitions, the company saw redundancies twice leaving a survival mode of thinking. The managers were then told that leadership was required throughout and a competency model was developed.

Leadership as a competency

The model was very good but the message now was, 'This is how we want you to behave', making compliance the driving force. The emphasis was still on strategic awareness and problem solving. Individuals were still not able to express their authentic leadership gifts. It was a case of, 'This is how we want leadership to look and how you'll be measured rather than personal growth and development.' Jay Conger studied AT&T in the USA and found that competency models here and in other companies were based on maintaining the hierarchy rather than developing leaders. Competency models according to Conger 'try to bring about an "ideal" state of leadership which few can attain'.[3]

Leadership and position

The biggest challenge for the financial company in the UK was with its senior managers. People looked to these individuals for guidance on behaviour and saw the old culture remaining. This means that the best leadership training is limited in its effect as delegates return to an organization still entrenched in rewarding targets, regardless of how they were achieved. Authentic leadership was suppressed while management thrived. The structure of the company is still a hierarchy that needs management to maintain it and where leadership is perceived as position for the few.

A similar story was found in the public sector. Leadership development for local government managers was offered to the top three tiers of managers. This included the chief executives and the two layers below. Much of the programme was based on psychological assessment and feedback. Mentoring was offered for a year after this and a work-based project completed the programme. Some of the delegates couldn't find a suitable mentor or didn't want one, as having one was perceived by some individuals to be a weakness.

Similarly in the NHS, leadership training has been offered to chief executives – separate from others; while senior managers are given leadership as part of management programmes. At the end of the day, the programmes had some development benefits but did the individuals develop their leadership potential? The answer was very few in a limited way. Leadership in parts of the public sector is being taught as a bolt-on to management and the 'vision' bit.

Out-of-date theory

Another issue for developing leaders is one where delegates are taught out-of-date ideas on leadership. The main reason for this is that the programmes are in reality management development with a 'leadership' label. These tend to last a week, during which delegates are taught up to 15 skills. Within this mass is 'leadership'. This is very common practice and is based on seeing leadership as an addition to management. An example of this perception is included in a letter sent by a senior civil servant in the UK, based at the Department of Education and Employment. It reads, 'There is no doubt that leadership is a vital element of management competence.'[4]

Leadership in the civil service, no matter what words they speak, is based on position in a hierarchy and this is reinforced in their thinking, policy and actions. An example of this is how the Department of Education and Employment has focused only on head teachers for leadership development.

Doing the job

Another approach to developing leadership is based on 'learning on the job'. The managing director of a company boasted to me how he had only ever attended one training course and that was years ago. He had learned everything he knew doing the job and now he was in his late fifties he wasn't going to learn anything new! Yet we know that this learning on the job is only part of what is required. Working day to day is a reactive process where individuals are busy doing and not allowing time for 'being' or reflecting on learning. These individuals at the top of hierarchies are watched closely by others in the organization. They give out powerful messages which include 'I don't need personal development and growth – that's for the rest of you.'

Spreading leadership

Some companies in the USA and their UK counterparts have tried to achieve a wider range of activities to develop leadership. Linked to their business strategy, leadership is perceived as enabling the company to provide the best service and ultimately improve its profits. Included in this strategy is the human element; 'Becoming a place where we want to work' was on the leadership initiative at one well-known organization.[5] Leadership development here included training, seminars, surveys, 360-degree feedback, mentoring, coaching and diversity studies. This holistic approach to development seems impressive but what has been the outcome? There was still a feeling of compliance – this is how leadership should look, this is how we want our employees to behave. The holistic development approach came over from the USA and there was a feeling among UK counterparts that tolerance of another culture would not be accepted.

At a well-known US computer company in the UK, many of the female employees said they would like to express their leadership but they felt blocked by their managers who were predominantly male. These managers were their biggest barrier to being able to become the authentic leaders they wanted to be. Exploring this further it was found that senior women managers played out quite competitive, aggressive styles that enabled them to be acceptable for promotion. In other words, women could 'succeed' if they behaved in a certain way and expressed a certain 'leadership style'.

There are two issues here. The first is that the majority of women wanted to express their leadership differently to what was accepted in the culture. Second, these companies who were US in origin were trying to recreate the same culture including how leadership was expressed in other countries. This is an issue I found working with global companies. If a company is successful in the USA it tends to duplicate its methods elsewhere in the world. The underlying belief driving this is, 'we do it best and you must copy.' – an attitude affecting leadership development in companies based in other parts of the world. This begs the question: does leadership in one country work elsewhere? The answer is 'no'. Not only because of cultural differences but also because leadership is a personal expression and no two leaders have ever expressed it the same way – regardless of where they originated from.

In a US financial services company based in the UK, the culture was dynamic but again the women felt they couldn't express themselves as leaders. Also the more senior the women the more arrogant and aggressive they were. This was evident in the most senior who was in charge of human resources. The women just below were very different but didn't stay very long because they felt that compliance was the order. They have now left this company and have set up their own practice because they felt they were losing their identity and having to become a different kind of leader to who they really were. This is a growing trend among both men and women, but particularly so for women.

Therefore, although there has been a huge increase in leadership development, very little has actually changed and the emphasis has remained on compliance and fitting in. This is the fault of the organization that still propagates a 'management mindset'. Organizational structures, cultures and thinking are unable at present to enable people everywhere to use their leadership potential. To develop leaders everywhere will require structural and systemic transformation in both organizations and their thinking.

A different approach has developed in Jack Welch's organization based on leaders teaching others. Noel Tichy who worked with Welch expands this even further when he writes: 'To be an effective teacher, one needs to be a world-class learner.'[6] This is impossible if individuals are arrogant and think that learning is for the masses but not for themselves, which is often the case at board level in the UK.

Training can explain concepts at an intellectual level and can develop certain skills but in developing leadership much more is required. Developing self-awareness, recognizing behavioural issues, practising leadership and using creativity, imagination and your whole self is needed. Today this is almost impossible working in jobs that require the use of rigid management processes.

In addition the way leadership is taught relies very much on a traditional approach which is fine for teaching certain skills. Here left-hand brain activities are taught with a left-hand brain approach. However, leadership is more right- than left-hand brain and under-standing and developing leadership requires approaches which differ from the usual teaching methods of training organizations.

In 1998 research in the UK found that 60% of leadership develop-ment was done through 'taught' methods that included business school courses, in-house training, customized programmes and external programmes. Any form of experiential learning was only 15% and any form of coaching and mentoring was about 15%. These figures were from large companies who tend to be the most active in training. Therefore the method as well as the context of leadership development is out of touch. This was reinforced by other blockages that included: a selfish attitude and not caring for others; arrogance and a management mindset; hierarchical thinking and structures; cultures that focus on tasks and performance; and rigid processes, all of which prevent true leadership. The outcome is to keep people in a helpless state, spending their days avoiding responsibility.

Most organizations have failed to see that leadership is a personal expression and requires both individual development and organizational transformation. Therefore the activity has had minimum effect and little has changed. If we want to develop leaders everywhere another way is necessary that goes beyond training.

Beyond training

A fast-growing business based in Southampton and the Thames Valley in the UK is based on the beliefs of respect for the individual, service to the customer and the pursuit of excellence. These values are lived and expressed by all, including the directors, on a daily basis. Every employee feels they can express their individual leadership because the structure is more like 'a network of workers reaching out to all parts' rather than a hierarchy. People are given responsibility and trust. An example is where sales people are encouraged to operate as if it were their own business, making decisions and working as a team.

Leadership development is based on personal growth and has included experiencing the human spirit with a trip to the site of the D-Day landings where individuals walked along the beaches and visited the cemeteries. Other developments have included fun on treasure hunts while learning to work as teams.

One manager remarked, 'There are no job specs and everyone puts forward creative ideas. People can express themselves through forums and everyone is listened to. Here I have the freedom to express my leadership.' Another said, 'The thing you notice is that directors have ears and will act on things. They set an example by caring for us.'

Everyone in the company believes they can be leaders and colleagues are there to support them. Everyone feels they are working together in the same direction and are kept informed through open communication. Ideas come from all over the company including the new 16-year-old school leaver. Everyone is given responsibility and trust to do their work. Everyone has a plan of where they want to be in five years' time that is reviewed every six months, and support is given to help individuals achieve these goals.

One person who joined less than two years ago said, 'They definitely let you be the best you can be. I'm doing things I've never done before. I can attempt to do things on my own but have support when I need it. If I make a mistake I learn from it and make sure it doesn't happen again. This is very different from my last company, which is probably the largest in the computer industry. There I had to inform my boss every day what I was planning to do and any ideas I put forward were put down as I was told, "This is how we've done it for 15 years and will continue to do so."'

The customer service given by the company for the computer industry is reflected in the employees' positive attitudes and turnover is growing fast. When its technical support people went out into other companies they found that customers often expected to see a hierarchy. 'But there is none,' said an employee. 'We're not big on job titles here. It's a friendly, open atmosphere. I tend to take ownership of projects and the company allows that. Customers trust me and they'll get that trust and service from my colleagues.'

With nearly 200 employees, the company is determined to remain the same as they grow. For those of you who argue this would be impossible in a larger organization or global company, you could not be more wrong. For any organization could achieve this if they really wanted to. Size is not a barrier – but rigid structures and thinking in the minds of managers is. The transformation requires much more than training – in fact a training department may not even be necessary! The reality is the majority of our present organizations suppress leadership and this can be seen when we take a closer look. What is the problem with organizations today?

2

The Problems of Organizational Life Today

*A regime which provides human beings no deep reasons to care
about one another cannot long preserve its legitimacy.*

Richard Sennett

At the start of a new millennium we are faced with a series of
problems affecting organizations on a global scale. In fact we
hear the same comments from our business, political and public sector
organizations:

'We know we need to change out structure, but to what?'

'We know we need to stop working within functional operations or
separate government departments – but people won't cooperate.'

'We know we need to motivate a more educated workforce now
called "knowledge workers" – but how? When we spend money
training them they move on.'

'We know people want better healthcare, education and a reduction
in crime. Can't they see that we need time to do this?'

'The competition are getting smarter but we can't control the
strength of the pound.'

'We're in the top 100 so we must be doing the right things. Aren't
we clever? Let's keep doing the same things.'

'There is enormous pressure to improve performance so we keep cutting costs which means losing more people – but it is the easiest way.'

'We know there is a need to develop leaders throughout the organization, but training doesn't seem to change much.'

The more we study these all-too-often-heard comments, the more we come to realize that they are not isolated issues. In fact, the more we study the issues facing organizations everywhere today the clearer it becomes that they are different facets of one single crisis. *Organizations as they are at present subscribe to a reality inadequate to deal with a fast-changing, globally interconnected world. Within this environment leadership is suppressed and needs to be unleashed.*

Transformation is the biggest challenge

Why is transformation so difficult? Surely with all the change everyone has experienced in recent years we must be on the right path now? It is true we have experienced 20 years of constant change so far – but as yet real transformation eludes us. Most organizations have approached change as a technical challenge. True, lasting, deep transformation is the biggest and most persistent challenge for all organizations today. Two things seem to be holding us back: the thinking or mindset of the people at the top of those organizations and the fact that no one has shown what should replace traditional thinking. *Unleashing Leaders* will address this.

It is a fact that there is a growing global consciousness which is challenging how we presently run our world with a strong belief that it could be much better. To achieve this transformation we have to allow all human potential to flourish, and above all, creativity and leadership to develop everywhere.

At present most organizations are suppressing the leadership poten-tial of individuals through their structures, rigid processes and thinking. At the same time many of those at the top of the hierarchy or in positions of power are abusing their positions and feeding their own self-interest and goals. Some people may believe this to be natural survival of the fittest. I prefer to see it as a few behaving this way because they have been able to get away with it. The hierarchical structure allows abuse of position. Yet everything is about to change. Alvin and Heidi Tofler remarked in the New York Times, 'The old world map is obsolete – we are undergoing the deepest rearrangement of global power since the birth of industrial civilization.'[1]

As part of this transformation we need to challenge the present structures and organizations, to enable leadership to be expressed throughout. This is the crisis facing organizations. First let us take a close look at organizations and the people within them to establish evidence that the old way is collapsing. It begins here with the largest and most influential – business organizations.

Business organizations today

Business organizations are now power bases which influence most of our lives. Yet many of these large organizations have achieved as much as they can in their present state. Their structures, ways of working and reliance on satisfying the financial institutions are constraining them. They continue to restructure, downsize or merge and cut costs on a global scale. The traditional hierarchical organization – though much flatter – is now in deep trouble and is poorly equipped to respond to the new business needs at large today.

Businesses on a world scale face a paradox. With globalization they have unprecedented opportunities to expand into the new markets that have opened up new ways to reach customers such as via the Internet; while at the same time traditional markets are changing dramatically, shrinking or becoming intensely competitive. In addition, rising customer demand for quality products and services and reduced profit margins are causing pressures. Costs have to keep being cut to show healthy profits for shareholders.

The stock market has enormous influence on how companies behave. The most damaging effect is from short-term thinking, which affects not only the organization, but even the environment and the community. An example of this is the closing down of banks in villages across the UK. As a result, people are now going to the towns to get the cash they need and shopping while they are there. The growing outcome is small shops in villages struggling to survive. At the same time, instead of walking into the village, people use cars to get to the towns to do their shopping which means more pollution. The decisions businesses make have far-reaching impact.

The outcome from a decade of cost cutting has been what Gary Hamel calls 'corporate anorexia' or slimmer organizations. However, they may be slimmer but they are not necessarily fitter. A great deal of knowledge and experience has been lost with the 'fat'. Cutting jobs or selling parts of the business is an easier option for directors than increasing total income, which requires imagination and the targeting of opportunities. I believe the UK has often been tougher than other countries in its cost-cutting practices. We have created a generation of 'hatchet men' who may be efficient managers but do not show any leadership and vision when it comes to real change. The emphasis is on achieving targets and every employee is under pressure. Does it work?

Productivity

In the UK some of the largest and most successful companies have lower productivity than their rivals elsewhere in Europe, according to a report from the Department of Trade and Industry.[2] The report challenges the CBI view that if all UK companies performed as well as the leaders in their domestic sector they would be up to world standard. 'In benchmarking themselves against the best, British companies need to be aware of whether they should be looking primarily at the best of British, or to the best foreign companies for their inspiration', says the report.[3] In a global world, UK companies cannot compete just with themselves.

So why is productivity low in the UK? Many companies blame a skill shortage. Yet McKinsey in the UK found *management* a greater constraint on the productivity of British business than skill shortages.[4]

They found that managers extract little output from each hour their employees work. Why is this? The study says skill deficiencies are not the main explanation; for instance, Japanese car plants and US hotels in the UK achieve high productivity from often low-skilled workers. Another example of this is Nissan in Sunderland who in 1999 achieved the best productivity in Europe for the third year running; while Toyota in Derbyshire moved up to fifth place and Honda in Swindon were tenth according to figures from the *Economist* Intelligence Unit.[5]

Added to this, the report from McKinsey says UK management decisions often impede higher productivity. This is usually done through either procrastination or starting an initiative only to change their mind halfway through because other priorities overtake. The government will argue that if we trained our managers better things would improve – I believe the 'problem' is much deeper and stems from our culture, beliefs and thinking. Low productivity is an outcome.

Alan Briskin asks: 'Is ever-increasing productivity truly the answer to employment? If so, what are the human consequences of market economies' constantly vying for the greatest productivity at the lowest cost?'[6] During the 1990s large companies in every business sector eliminated around a quarter of their workforce and the trend continues today with the rise in mergers and acquisitions. All this comes under the auspices of 'change' while leadership remains dormant. Change has dominated organizations for several years.

Change

A 1999 survey carried out by the Institute of Management and the University of Manchester Institute of Science and Technology found that 61% of managers said their organizations carried out a change programme in the previous 12 months.[7] The most common forms were: cost reduction, redundancies, culture change and performance improvement. It is interesting to note how reaction to these varies: 79% of junior and 74% of middle managers thought morale in particular had suffered, compared with 60% of senior managers and *only* 21% of chief executives. The survey concluded: 'Change management has not generally had its intended consequences, while the blind pursuit of headcount reduction has adversely affected morale and perceptions of job security.'[8]

Downsizing continues

Restructuring is essentially a means to lay off managers and employees to reduce the hierarchy but not to change it. Do directors still sit up in their offices? The effects are still being felt and insecurity grows as a further phase of restructuring is running at the beginning of the twenty-first century. What has noticeably eroded in organizations is the trust that is fundamental to commitment and performance. Lack of trust affects the bottom line. In the 1990s studies from the American Management Association and Wyatt Consultants found that companies who had repeated downsizing produced lower profits and declining worker productivity.[9] At the same time, less than half these companies achieved the savings they had planned, fewer than one third increased profitability and less than one in four increased their productivity.

In the UK the downsizing continues. British Telecom have announced axing more than 3000 management jobs in a bid to cut costs. British Airways announce 6500 jobs to go in three years to reduce its costs by a further £600m. AXA the insurance company have also recently announced redundancies and BAe Systems have announced large redundancies following their merger with Marconi Systems. Countless examples can be drawn across all sectors of industry.

Everywhere individuals keep their heads down and hope they won't be next to face redundancy. Inside these organizations management keeps a hold while people give up their leadership for compliance. Routines, rigidity and control suppress initiative, ideas and energy. Instead the emphasis is on specialization, bureaucratic processes, political in-fighting and pressure from day-to-day problems. Alan Briskin concludes: 'Conformity is gained by way of appraisal systems and a tight corporate culture. Everyone feels watched and judged, even if the manager is less overtly controlling.'[10]

This was the case for the 4000 staff at 37 BT sites who deal with domestic telephone customers. They were threatening industrial action because they felt they were constantly watched and timed – even how long they spent in the lavatory. Stories of pregnant women being told they were going to the toilet too often filled newspapers with concern for how other call centres were being run. What have we become when people work under a regime of management out of a Dickensian age?

All organizations are struggling with greater demands from customers, new sources of competition, economic factors, advances in technology, globalization, or implementing initiatives such as performance-related pay; while employees are distrustful of more ideologies such as empowerment because they have proved to amount to worthless words.

It seems that in spite of having strategic planners and organizational development managers, the struggling continues and organizations are not being proactive. The majority of managers will say their work is mainly reactive, which may include dealing with a recent merger or responding to a competitor in another country. With an emphasis on reactive behaviour, real transformation will elude us and everyone remains busy dealing with 'problems'.

State of two minds

Birchall and Lyons from Henley Future Work Forum argue that reactive behaviour is performed only in response to the actions of others.[11] They go on to introduce the concept of the 'tactile' organization. This is an organization which can see, hear, analyse and even understand what is required – but cannot act. Instead it is what Birchall and Lyons describe as a 'state of two minds' which is demonstrated by the outlook of different individuals. One mind will see opportunities and want to change; the other mind is risk-averse and unable to confront its own inadequacies. This means that the organization both 'knows' and 'does not want to know' depending on who you are talking to. So how does this sort of organization move forward?

Birchall and Lyons argue that in order to act the organization has to believe there is a need to change that comes from direct experience, which it will 'feel'. Often this means the organization must feel pain to enable it to learn and act. Yet avoiding pain is a human reaction that can lead to neglecting any learning required for the new world emerging. An example of this recently came from a leadership programme for some senior individuals. Most took the learning on board even though they knew on returning to work it would be difficult to implement. However, a handful and in particular one delegate refused to participate and just kept saying the time spent on the course was pointless as he wasn't going to change from how he had always behaved and worked. This man was afraid of facing the truth of how he impacted on others – the learning was too painful. Instead he put up a huge barrier and disrupted others on his team.

Learning

Lack of learning in organizations is also affecting opportunities to be gained from technology especially at board level. In an Institute of Directors/Bathwick Group survey it was found only 64% of UK directors use computers at work, compared with 84% of German directors and 100% of those in Japan and Singapore.[12] The director-general of the IoD said: 'There is mounting evidence that our business leaders do not understand information technology. They would prefer to have little to do with it.'[13]

He said too many directors were 'dangerously outmoded and complacent about IT'. Such executives he likened to 'Neanderthals', 'slow-witted and quite unable to compete with more adaptive, versatile competitors', Philip Crawford, senior vice president of Oracle, the software group, added his voice saying the UK treated IT as an administrative overhead. He added: 'Such wilful ignorance and complacency are tantamount to corporate negligence.'[14]

Yet the notion of learning is changing from job skills that require periodic updating to the mindset of lifelong learning which is a continuous process. It is interesting that gender influences personal development. A study by the Small Business Research Trust showed that female managers seeking additional training outside the office gave IT their top priority whereas male managers rated marketing training.[15]

In large organizations today another form of learning has emerged. To survive, people 'learn' to keep their heads down and keep personal initiative to a minimum. How common is this type of learning process?

Two types of employees

According to neurolinguistic programming (NLP) practitioners there seem to be two types of people in the world: those who love their work, see it as an extension of themselves, read books and journals to keep up with ideas in their field and 'play' with their work even when at home relaxing. These people are passionate about what they do and are what is known as 'associated' with their work.

Then there are those who separate their working life from their private life; their work is not an extension of themselves but rather more likely to be just a job. At work they do what is asked and no more. These individuals are what is known as 'disassociated' with their work. When people are disassociated from their work, they are detaching themselves from any emotions or feelings about the work and their role.

Coping at work

However, there are millions of people who are disassociated with their work, not by personal choice, but as a way of surviving organizational life, its politics and backstabbing. In other words, disassociation has become a strategy, a way of coping and living in organizations, particularly large ones. This behaviour seems to be more common in the public sector where dismissal is very slow and individuals have to survive a boss who is a very poor manager.

A coping strategy exists at senior management level too where individuals have the power to change their working lives but choose not to. A survey carried out by the Industrial Society and Resource Connection (a consultancy specializing in helping companies introduce flexible working) found that although 80% of executives wanted more flexibility and 42% were unhappy with their work/life balance, they would not change anything.[16] The reason for this is that the managers (all male in the survey) feared that it would result in their being perceived as less of 'the company man' ideal and might lead to 'career death'. Working less is seen as the 'female' option and as such the executives would not change the long-hours culture for themselves or others. When these executives become directors, they will expect the same from their managers. This scenario is the start of a vicious circle and a self-perpetuating problem.

These mindsets and thinking are holding us back and causing strain and stress. How can leadership develop in this environment?

Smaller businesses

Meanwhile the number of smaller businesses is growing – especially dot.coms – and they are attracting graduates who would once have concentrated on the large corporate milk round. A study of Harvard Business School alumni revealed that 20 years after graduation, most had defected to small, entrepreneurial concerns or were in service industries such as consulting or banking.[17] Research by Catalyst in New York showed that women managers tend to leave large companies, not for other blue-chip jobs, but to start their own business because they are fed up with the corporate world.[18] This trend is growing in the UK.

Case study

Vanessa was a human resources director in the computer industry working for a large global corporation. Her story is one I've heard many times.

The positive things about working in a large organization are the companionship of others, the comradeship and network opportunities. You work with a broad section of people who come and go, which is a challenge. Of course there is also the regular pay cheque and career opportunities because you build credibility and people know you.

However, a corporate doesn't look out for its people in a proactive role, identifying who the people with strengths are and helping them so they can be useful across the whole corporation. As a woman it can feel there is a glass ceiling and you have to keep redefining and re-establishing yourself to constant new bosses. There needs to be a long-term vision at the top to enable everyone to work effectively but instead different things start with no follow-through.

As a woman in a male-dominated environment I had to prove myself to be better and smarter than everyone else. It's a challenge working for people who are not always up to the job. Each new managing director would change direction so you were constantly working on behalf of someone else while trying to achieve something. There are lots of levels of hierarchy with people unwilling to change – the blockers who said all the right words but did not take the action. Those at the top knew who they were but didn't do anything about it. It was, 'We know best, just do your job.' Then there was the politics and lack of support that create the barriers that result in organizations falling apart. These cracks are becoming visible through the advances of IT.

Although it's early days in working for myself it's now down to me. It's my reputation and I'm only as good as my last assignment without the protection of a regular pay cheque, but I have the motivation from companies who want you to go in and help them. I don't get involved with the hierarchical struggles or politics, or think I'll upset someone, which could cost me promotion. Instead I can give objective feedback and because they are paying for me I can get the attention needed from the right people. I see things being achieved at a faster pace. In smaller organizations there is no need for the continual consultation on everything. Decision-making is much quicker because there are fewer managers and they listen. You can get people to think instead of being tied to processes that are still hierarchical. The corporates may have flatter structures but the processes have led them to recreating what they have removed. It is still hierarchical.

The big change is the e revolution, which affects our everyday life and has become a lifeline for me personally. It speeds up everything – the pace of decision-making, information flow – and things will never go back to how they were; it will only get faster. I see others being left behind. For example, it's ripping the heart out of the financial organizations who are going to have to reduce their staff and change the way they work. The days of the large corporations are numbered.

Outside the corporate world you realize how much everything costs and the sheer waste in executive travel and expensive hotels that large companies pay for. It isn't necessary today. You can make decisions through email rather than fly off to other parts of the world. Managers are slow to embrace this and so we continue to pollute the roads and skies. Managers have blissful unawareness of costs, and when it comes to changing for environmental reasons the view is 'great idea, but not in my backyard'. Instead they play the 'being present' game of turning up at 7.30 a.m. and leaving at 7.30 p.m. because they believe this will make them a high achiever.

Would I go back? Wild horses couldn't drag me. I'm intrigued with what's happened to me – I've changed already and want to see where this change is taking me. A big salary would not entice me – there's more to life and money doesn't make you happy. In the corporate world you get a pair of velvet handcuffs and the next thing is you are there ten years later. I have no regrets that I left.

Support for entrepreneurs

If this is a growing trend what sort of support can individuals get to start working for themselves? According to the *London Business School Global Entrepreneurship Monitor*, only 16% of Britons think there are good start-up opportunities compared to 57% in the USA.[19] The LBS study shows the main causes for the difference between the two nations are both cultural and social and they are partly the product of an anti-capitalist education system in the UK. The report demonstrated that entrepreneurship is linked to economic growth. In the USA 70% of the 18 million new jobs created since 1993 have come from new businesses.

Women are leading the way after leaving corporate world. Small and medium-size businesses run by women alone now account for more jobs than the Fortune 500 top companies. Lloyds TSB in the UK have undertaken research of a sample of 14 100 companies set up in 1998 and found that of the 191 that achieved a turnover in excess of £1 million in 1999 half were run by women.[20] Thus a similar trend to that in the USA is emerging in the UK.

The *Global Entrepreneurship Monitor* research also found that 95% of adults in the USA respected entrepreneurs, compared with 75% in France and Germany. In Britain, only 30% showed respect for entrepreneurs. In the UK the status of those working for large companies is much higher. Will this change in the future? It will if the number of entrepreneurs grows.

Two scenarios

The Department of Trade and Industry has looked into the future and outlines two possible scenarios for the UK in 2015.[21] The first is called Wired World and depicts an economy composed of a network of individuals working and communicating through the Internet. Here, 40% of people work for themselves, in an economy driven by entrepreneurial business start-ups. Large corporations have been replaced by a resurgence of guilds and trade associations that provide a social network.

The second scenario is called Built to Last and assumes the economy develops in the opposite direction. Large corporations dominate the scene as employers compete with each other to retain their employees, whose knowledge is seen as their competitive advantage. In this environment technology improvements, globalization and the speed at which information is disseminated are colluding to rob established groups at their edge. Even the economies of scale that once favoured large companies are no longer as compelling, since technology has dramatically pushed down overhead costs.

More initiatives

Inside organizations further 'initiatives' are announced – such as improvements through coaching or customer care – while production processes and computerization are updated. However, these have had mixed results. Research by Ashridge found that 70% of chief executives felt that total quality management (TQM) had failed to fulfil its promise within two years of the beginning of the initiative.[22] Whereas business process re-engineering resulted in disillusionment and confusion, often with a compromise for the part of the organization being re-engineered. Or, even worse, the organization itself was re-engineered with the exclusion of top management.

The fault does not always lie with some of the change initiatives themselves, but rather how they are implemented. Also the traditional structure of organizations cannot accommodate the suggested changes the initiatives need. You can hear executives saying there *has* been revolutionary change but Koch and Godden say: 'We have spent the past quarter century working as executives and consultants in large corporations, and we can confirm the absence of revolution or even radical change.'[23]

Internal demands of the hierarchy

In the meantime managers spend more and more time addressing internal demands. A survey carried out by Koch and Godden found that 60% of senior managers' time is spent on internal matters, mainly reacting to past events.[24] This retrospection leads to senior managers seeking to establish to whom blame should be apportioned as well as 'fixing things'. This in turn reinforces 'survival' behaviour rather than the expression of leadership or creativity.

While the recognition that we need to behave differently is just beginning, the world remains wired in a way that encourages old behaviours. An example is the story of the queues of people seen outside UK passport offices during the summer of 1999. IT industry experts argued that placing the blame on 'technical' problems only concealed the real cause – poor management, inadequate training and insufficient staff. David Taylor, president of the Association of IT Directors, says it is management, not staff, who are at fault. 'People don't want to be accountable or take ownership of the project. In the public sector heads don't roll as early as they would in the private sector. Someone has to accept the blame and then start to sort it out.[25]

Today managers are realizing that all the present initiatives cannot solve the problems. They are struggling and frustrated with all the meetings they feel they need to attend. 'Corporations talk about reshaping themselves,' says Harvard professor Rosabeth Moss Kanter, 'but mostly it's just talk.'[26]

Managerial mediocrity

Abraham Zaleznik from Harvard feels we are 'adrift in a sea of managerial mediocrity, desperately needing leadership to face worldwide economic competition'.[27] Warren Bennis tells the story of a scientist at the University of Michigan who made a list of what he saw as the greatest dangers to society. Third on the list was the quality of management and leadership in our institutions! How can this be possible after a quarter of a century of management training and a huge increase in business graduates from universities?

Talent

An *Economist* Intelligence Unit/Hewett Associates report in 1998 looked at recruiting management talent in 150 large international companies.[28] More than one third of the companies described finding and retaining talent and a lack of management capabilities as the greatest obstacle to growth – which after 30 years of management development seems illogical. Why is this such a problem? According to the report, it is due to a lack of commitment by senior management to such issues as employee communications and creating a social atmosphere among employees.

Although the research revealed a desire among many big companies to offer 'well paid, rewarding, fulfilling work and a chance to develop in a pleasant working environment', few know how to achieve this. 'Giant multinationals and brain-heavy high-technology corporations alike keep stumbling in their attempt to achieve the balance of cash and culture that is required,' says the report. 'Breaking into new business, entering new markets, managing joint ventures, and making acquisitions and alliances work requires multiskilled general managers with track records,' the report reads.[29] Many of these were shed during the downsizing and restructuring and still it continues. Have business organizations kicked themselves in the foot? Or is the problem management itself?

Management is about order

The way organizations are managed around routines, rigidity and control seems to suppress initiative, ideas and energy. There is a belief that if we exert more control, we'll achieve the results we need. Therefore the emphasis is on specialization and bureaucratic processes. Organizations today are full of ladders which go to dead ends; high levels of stress while trust has sunk to the ground; where the mentality is 'everyone for themselves' and the emphasis on cost reduction.

There is talk of cross-functional teamwork but the tendency in most cases is to manage organizations by separating them into parts. Organizations say they have become matrix structures with self-managed teams. These teams do not need managing but there is perceived a need to put managers into them. The answer has been for the teams to be given team leaders who were the managers!

Keeping organizations under control, particularly the costs, has become the primary challenge. The rise in shareholder value as the dominant driving force in business has resulted in a total lack of sensitivity to basic human values. So attention turns inward and management is institutionalized into the culture. Organizations employ people whose main role is to manage the internal processes, i.e. maintain the structure and system and keep things as they are. Sometimes the methods used by a few individuals are quite shocking.

Bullying

Research supported by the TUC and CBI found that nearly half of the employees questioned had witnessed bullying at work and one in ten had been bullied within the past six months.[30] This was the largest survey undertaken by UMIST. It found bullying was most common in the prison service and the post and telecommunications sector, where 16% of respondents had been bullied within the previous six months. Other professions that rate highly in the bullying stakes are teaching with 15.5% and the performing arts with 14%.

One in ten senior managers – who were the most common perpetrators – said he or she had been bullied. There seems to be a pattern that if someone is bullied there will be a tendency to copy. There is still at large the belief that the only way to get people to work hard is to shout and dominate them. This is surprising after 40 years of management training which includes managing people. Therefore is the behaviour of managers dependent on the work they do and the roles they have, or is there something more worrying about the vast number of managers created over the last 50 years?

Work of managers

It was Henry Mintzberg who first accurately described managers work in 1973 when he wrote: 'the executives I was studying . . . were fundamentally indistinguishable from their counterparts of 100 years ago . . . Their decisions concern modern technology, but the procedures they use are still the same as . . . [those of] the nineteenth-century manager.' This continues today in many organizations although it is denied. Koch and

Godden argue that managed organizations are still bureaucracies dedicated to organizing, administration and planning rather than doing things. Robert Heller says: 'The prime myth of management is that it does.'[31] This can be backed up by the fact that downsizing can still continue without affecting operations.

Koch and Godden show that instead of serving the interests of customers, managers serve the interests of managers either as individuals or as a class.[32] They argue that this behaviour is not necessarily a conscious reaction. It happens because of the structure and method of operating in organizations. Along with the unconscious behaviour is what I call the 'management mindset' or thinking which is a remnant of the Industrial Revolution yet to be completely transformed. This mindset is based on a way of seeing the world, and present organizational structures maintain this thinking. In this environment it is impossible for leaders to thrive.

Need for revitalization and leadership

What is becoming clear is that we do not need to undertake further downsizing (often called 'restructuring') or rationalizing of organizations; instead we need to revive and revitalize them to enable leadership to be expressed throughout. The question remains, how? What is clear is that we cannot continue as we have and that the seriousness in the decline of organizations we saw in the 1990s was a global phenomenon that affected organizations everywhere. The next chapter shows the extent of the problem, sector by sector; profession after profession; and tries to show why there has been such a growing need for leadership, particularly in the last decade.

3

The Good, the Bad and the Ugly

As you look at the individuals who are in major positions of influence upon our planet you can see whether or not they are succeeding in their tasks of advancing humanity by the choices that they make . . . They have chosen . . . to represent a system that is disintegrating, and so their own systems are disintegrating before their eyes.

Gary Zukav

The last 20 years saw a decline in trust, accountability and leadership at the same time there has been a rise in self-interest, greed and dishonesty by those who exploited the culture and politics of the 1980s. In this environment it is very difficult, maybe impossible, for leaders to be unleashed. The evidence of this decline is everywhere.

In this chapter we will see how difficult it has been to develop leadership in specific industry sectors and in parts of the communities we live in. If we really want to unleash leaders everywhere we have to tackle these issues rather than rely on training.

Profit vs trust

Trust within financial institutions has been an issue in the UK with the mis-selling of pensions. Sales people sold unsuitable pensions designed to maximize their commissions at the expense of the investors. This process was set up by management and so they are accountable. One of the regulators, the Financial Services Authority (FSA) heavily criticized Prudential Assurance in particular not only for mis-selling, but also for dragging their heels in doing anything about it. The FSA stated that the Prudential had 'a deep-seated and long-standing failure in management', that prevented it from 'recognizing its own shortcomings', and had a 'cultural disposition against compliance'.[1]

How did these financial companies and shareholders in general gain the power they hold today? The answer has more to do with politics than business. When President Reagan took office in the USA he blamed the government for the mess the country found itself in. He supported allowing the 'market' to drive the economy.

At this time there were about 50 large corporations such as IBM, Procter and Gamble and 3M who controlled business with shareholders who were relatively weak. Among these 50 were older corporations who ran their businesses like families with a patriarchal environment and who became vulnerable to individuals such as Goldsmith from the UK. He and others were hired to begin hostile takeovers of some of these US companies and cut them to a minimum until their performance looked good. As a result shareholders and the market became the winners.

Support for the raiders

Those managing pension funds had to decide whether to support these new 'raiders' as they were known. The financial companies took their role of getting the best return for pensions literally and supported the raiders. Thatcher was impressed and followed the ideas, making her comment: 'Capitalism created wealth for the many not the few.'[2] Downsizing began in the UK and while thousands lost their jobs, profits increased. The reality was a situation where a few individuals were getting very rich, particularly the banks. Directors of pension funds stuck to their role as keepers of high returns and didn't see anything immoral about what was happening.

Suddenly the few who were gaining were showing signs of corruption as insider trading was unmasked in the UK and cases such as the Guinness bid for Distillers became media headlines. Eventually, the founder of this financial revolution in the USA was arrested for insider dealing and corruption. Others like Goldsmith were given knighthoods by Thatcher. Pension funds took power and became raiders themselves. At the same time, corruption in British politics began to raise its head as favours to boards of companies and parliamentary questions for money became known. The battle between the government and the 'market' resulted in high interest rates which affected thousands of home buyers. GATT and Maastricht trade agreements were seized as they enabled factories to be built in parts of the world where employment was cheap. Globalization began and the economy worldwide eventually became unstable resulting in the global economic crisis. Is the financial world all negative?

Social responsibility

The last few years has seen a growth in 'ethical' investment and a more socially responsible attitude among fund managers. Ethical investments have fared better over the past decade according to a *Sunday Times* study carried out in July 2000.[3] The average ethical fund had grown by 159% since 1990 and 115% since 1995. Today pension fund managers are being told to consider the 'environmental, social and ethical' implications of companies they invest in. The *Sunday Times* revealed that 21 out of the 25 biggest pension funds will be introducing an ethical investment policy. Interestingly, these successful ethical funds are often run by women in the City who are growing in number. Change for better is coming.

Rip-off Britain

Trust, accountability, lack of leadership and greed have also become issues in other financial organizations. With building societies becoming banks, reports on mis-selling mortgages have emerged. In 1999 Chancellor Brown tackled the issue of mortgages sold by banks and building societies by laying down new rules. This followed lenders not passing on interest rate cuts to borrowers when they fell. The Consumers' Association went further and named the Halifax, Abbey National and Northern Rock as the worst offenders.[4]

In March 2000 Don Cruickshank published his review of the UK banks.[5] The largest four were accused of abusing their position to make excessive profits at the expense of retail and business customers. This he claimed had come about because of lack of competition, resulting in personal customers and small businesses providing the profits to the banks. However, Mr Cruickshank went further and stated that the fault also lay with the regulatory system which allowed banks to get away with it. All this has led to the question being asked: what happened to business ethics?

Ethics in practice

In the mid-1990s, the University of Westminster carried out a survey on business ethics in Britain.[6] It found that although business people displayed a high degree of ethical awareness, many would jettison their principles if they affected their company's profitability. The research showed an ethical separation between senior managers and their junior staff and women who were more concerned about the environment, staff relations and trade with countries that abused human rights. Things are changing as these issues have become high profile.

In the USA, large corporates have created a new manager – the ethics officer – charged with ensuring corporate probity. These individuals are often law graduates who oversee business ethics. Their role is usually to develop an ethical code of conduct, and to set up an ethics programme for employees and a telephone hotline. In 1999 research by Arthur Andersen in six large US companies found that having a code of conduct and telephone hotline had the least impact on staff behaviour.[7]

Far more important was whether staff believed senior management adhered to and valued ethical behaviour as much as improving the bottom line. In fact the report argues that it may be more harmful to have an ethics and compliance programme, the existence of which employees perceive is only to protect the reputation of top management, than to have no programme at all. The European approach, which involves building an environment or culture within an organization that enables people to act with integrity, is far better.

An excuse not to develop a culture of integrity often cited by employees is that they are only behaving like their bosses. In the UK the controversy over high boardroom pay will not go away and still companies are failing to address it. If this is corporate leadership do we want more of it elsewhere?

A story of business 'leaders'

In 1992, the first UK report[8] on board reform, which was convened under the chairmanship of Sir Adrian Cadbury, former chairman of Cadbury Schweppes, came up with the following recommendations:

- A balance of power at the top of companies, preferably through a separate chairman and chief executive;
- At least three independent, non-executive directors;
- Formal nomination and selection procedures for non-executives;
- Remuneration committees to set pay of executive directors;
- Maximum three-year contracts;
- Fuller pay disclosure for chairmen and highest paid directors, especially of bonuses;
- Audit committees to aid independence of auditors and ensure effective internal controls.

Three researchers from Dundee University found a 'significant positive market reaction' when the jobs of CEO and chairman were separated. In the year following the separation of the posts, performance improved.[9] Sensible corporate governance is good for business.

This seemed a good start to reforming boards and the work continued, this time under the chairmanship of Sir Richard Greenbury, chairman of Marks and Spencer.[10] The proposals announced in 1995 were:

- Remuneration committee to report separately from the board;
- Details to include full pay and bonuses for each director, including pensions;
- Greater emphasis on long-term bonus schemes rather than options and annual bonuses, to be voted on by shareholders;
- Bonuses should be based on demanding performance criteria;
- Directors' pay increases should be 'sensitive' to pay rises elsewhere in the company.

Despite this, in most companies, the reality has been directors giving themselves high pay rises. The only difference is that we know about it now. This is because the third and final report in 1997 under the chairmanship of Sir Ronnie Hampel produced a backlash to the work begun with the Cadbury Report. It gave broad approval of present boardroom practice, saying that directors' main responsibility was to shareholders.[11]

In reviewing how previous corporate governance rules were being implemented Sir Ronnie Hampel said: 'The balance has been too much directed at accountability and not enough at prosperity and I am eager to see the balance corrected.'[12] He rejected any moves to let shareholders vote on directors' pay and added that boards should not be constrained by rigid rules. Therefore the recommendations were:

- Boards should assess directors' collective and individual performance;
- At least a third of the board should be non-executive;
- Non-executive directors can be paid in shares;
- Rejection of lighter rules for smaller companies;
- Rejection of shareholder votes on directors' remuneration policies and packages;
- Rejection of compulsory voting by institutions;
- Separation of chair and chief executive preferable, but not essential.

It was two steps forward and three steps back for boardroom ethics, giving a message to employees that ethics does not have a place in business organizations. In such an environment developing leadership on training courses is very limited because those who should be mentors – the board – were behaving contrary to what would be learned in the training rooms.

Further expectations

In 1998, boardroom pay escalated again – only this time it led to sharp criticism and the government looked at possible legislation to give shareholders more control over what directors earn. Many received increases of over 100% while nurses were given a 2.5% increase. Overall, top directors in Britain's 350 largest quoted companies pay packages rose 17.8% in 1998 with nearly 10% of CEOs receiving basic pay rises of 25% or more. The highest paid directors now collect as much in a working week as the average employee earns in a year. This follows the Chancellor saying in his budget speech a few months earlier: 'It would be the worst of short-termism to pay ourselves more today at the cost of higher interest rates, fewer jobs and slower growth tomorrow. All of us must therefore show greater responsibility.[13]

High boardroom pay continued in 1999 and doesn't appear to be slowing down. On top of this, bonuses for some FTSE 100 bosses can be worth more than half of their salaries even if their company's performance just stands still. Therefore, tying pay to share increases is inaccurate. A ten-year study in the USA shows that only 30% of share movement is a reflection of corporate performance, with 70% driven by market sentiment.[14] All this has now driven Stephen Byers, the Secretary of State for Trade and Industry, to announce that shareholders can vote on the board remuneration report for publically quoted companies. However, the change takes the form of a written code of practice rather than legislation.

When looking at directors' pay packages, one of the issues is how to measure performance. This is not just what is the best measure of value to the shareholder, but rather what combination of performance measures adequately reflects a given executive's contribution.

Performance

PricewaterhouseCoopers brought out a report in 1999 on pay and performance in Britain's 500 largest firms, which showed a critical need for performance measures.[15] However, the report editor found that shareholders were not interested in directors' pay. It seems that for many shareholders, as long as their shares are earning money for them, the question of how the business is run is not an issue. That attitude is now changing among shareholders. So again we are on the cusp of change.

Prime Minister Blair attempted to urge top executives to moderate pay rises but was not listened to. At least seven of the already highest paid executives in Britain's 100 largest companies were given pay rises of more than 50% in 1999. The average pay was £826 000 which is £16 000 every week – which is what many earn in a year. Is this fair? What does this say about leadership based on position?

Some have tried to justify the increases by saying the rises are necessary in a global competitive environment and without these salaries we will lose good executives. However, UK executives are paid the highest in Europe while the workforce are paid the lowest. Oxford economist Peter Oppenheimer remarked in *Management Today*: 'This global senior executives marketplace argument is an absolute nonsense . . . Even inside Europe, the recruitment of senior executives across boarders is still almost unheard of.'[16] The only country that gives higher wages to executives is the USA.

Corporate responsibility

In 1998, President Clinton had breakfast with 100 chief executives to urge them to fulfil their 'corporate responsibility' to workers. He urged them to create 'family friendly' workplaces and to adopt as their motto: 'Do well by doing good.'[17] It was interesting that the Republicans criticized this as 'evidence of this administration's desire to control the economy', thus giving the corporate world justification for not changing as the change was linked to government 'meddling'. In a similar way the

UK government has been accused of 'meddling' in how companies run themselves when they have suggested changes. Today those running the top telecoms, food retailing and banking in the UK are starting to feel a backlash from their shareholders who have had enough of big bonus payouts.

Another problem for the British government is that they have ruled out any increase in the 40% top rate of income tax and have so far refused to force shareholders to vote on all directors' pay packages at annual meetings or to insist on linking pay and performance. These overpaid directors are benefitting from the British tax system which compared to the US is 50.81%, France 54%, Stockholm 55%, Germany 56% and Japan 65%. This extra tax could help with education and health in the UK. So why has pay increased so much?

One reason why directors pay themselves so much is because they can. They do not own the company but they control its resources. Being in charge of money that belongs to someone else presents the temptation to take what you can. The present emphasis on shareholder value has led to many company directors being not so much interested in providing quality products and services or providing a long-term future for the company as in delivering improved value to shareholders which they see as a higher share price.

More accountability

Performance of directors must be made more accountable. Railtrack made huge profits because the Department for Transport rushed through the sale and undervalued it, enabling directors to have large bonuses. Today, Railtrack earns more than £1 million a day yet has failed to invest in a responsible way in its very old system of public transport. At the same time, the Health and Safety Executive report in 1999 warned that the 'margin of safety was being eroded'.[18]

What is clear is that salary has become the status symbol of the corporate director and more so for the global corporate director. This self-interested greed also reflects the short-term thinking of their business strategies. The professional manager has replaced the leader and now cries of 'where are the leaders in business?' abound.

In the last couple of years there have been several companies in the top 200 who have had a problem finding a chief executive. If individuals drive for more and more material wealth, they will find that those around them and attracted to them are the same self-interested individuals. The length of service in the role is also shortening. Already in the USA nearly half the current CEOs in the largest 476 corporations have been in post for less than three years. In addition, during the last five years, two thirds of all US companies have installed new CEOs. The expectations are high when pay is high on individuals who as yet have not learned to share power or build teams. This is not true leadership, but it is what individuals below see as leadership in a hierarchy.

Statistics rule

In the meantime, the public sector has been obsessed with numbers and quantity so their political masters can stand up in the House of Commons and spout statistics that tell nothing about quality. The issues are not about more arrest warrants issued in the police service or hospital beds filled in hospitals but less crime and better health.

US writer Daniel Quinn says that the reason why the public sector fails to improve many social situations is because they take a 'military' approach.[19] Examples include 'war' on poverty, 'war' on drugs, 'fight' crime, 'combat' homelessness, 'defeat' AIDS, 'defeat' hunger. Quinn says that engineers can teach us something here. When dealing with overwhelming forces, Quinn shows how engineers using accedence to resistance rather than force are more effective. Instead of strong rigid buildings, flexible ones are more effective in earthquakes. In social issues we should acknowledge the issues and those surrounding them rather than fight them. In other words: approach issues with different thinking.

This begs the question: can we change the thinking in present organizations while they remain hierarchical with 'management' throughout? In some of the public sector there is low morale and little motivation among people. Young graduates join with high expectations and enthusiasm which gradually wears down. A 'blame culture' often abounds with everyone blaming other people, the system, lack of resources and so on. Leadership is almost non-existent. Within this culture, accountability and responsibility are failing the public at large.

Public sector money

On 1 December 1999 the Audit Commission published figures that showed a large increase in public sector fraud.[20] The figure accrued was £108 million. The report 'Protecting the Public Purse' showed that councils in England and Wales detected £104 million in illegal payments, while fraud in the NHS doubled to £4.7 million. For the first time corrupt GPs were included in the statistics. Fraud by GPs, dentists, opticians and pharmacists has trebled, yet only 25 doctors have been charged and dismissed, while illegal claims from opticians rose from £31 000 in 1996–1997 to £1.3 million in 1998–1999. The behaviour from other organizations seems to be spreading, making it difficult for leadership to be unleashed.

Culture of early retirement

Recently, the UK government launched a review into public sector early retirement which is costing the taxpayers £1 billion a year.[21] This followed a series of cases where public employees were found to have taken large pension payouts even though they seemed perfectly healthy. One example is of a police officer who ran a marathon despite having been declared unfit to face a disciplinary enquiry into allegations of corruption. Sir Paul Condon, the Metropolitan Police Commissioner, has publicly noted that between 1995 and 1996, more than 70% of officers facing investigation or disciplinary charges retired on medical grounds.

Overall, in the five years up to 1997, 73% of all fire officers, 49% of police, 33% of NHS staff, 23% of teachers and 22% of civil servants retired on grounds of ill health. In some local councils, more than half of all staff retire early, whereas in others the rate is 10%.

Lord MacKenzie, a former head of the Police Superintendents' Association, said that the culture of compensation is enfeebling the police, creating officers who think only about filling their bank balances rather than performing their duties. Although this has been the behaviour of a few it sends out a negative message to the rest of the force. In this environment it is impossible for people to feel valued and respected and for leadership to thrive.

Gender still an issue?

Being valued is also a gender issue when half the population is devalued in pay just because of their sex. Even with changes in legislation and cultural changes in society at large it is still the case that men are paid more than women for the same or similar jobs. Female doctors, pharmacists and lecturers are paid up to one fifth less than their male counterparts. The median pay for male civil servants stands at £19 000 compared with £14 000 for women according to Incomes Data Services. Women in banking, finance and insurance earn just 55.6% of the wage paid to their male counterparts.

Male academics at almost every university and college in the UK are paid more than women. The exceptions are Glasgow College of Art and King Alfred's College, Winchester. The largest discrepancy is at the London Business School where men earn an average of almost £20 000 a year more. Top medical schools that have traditionally been male-dominated head the list of institutions with the greatest pay gap. It is clear that there is still prevailant in society the message that men are worth more than women.

In 1997 Labour won the election because Tony Blair won the support of women. Electoral success had eluded Labour for many years because they couldn't get support from women who favoured the Tories.

Why did they switch? There were two reasons: the first was that women preferred Labour's policies; and second, Labour seemed to be committed to bringing women into the political arena and government. There was an expectation that at last politics itself might change and leadership could be expressed by more women in the field of politics.

Women voters

Today there has been a turnaround in Labour's popularity and it is women who are the most dissatisfied with the government. At work women are aware of the lack of women in senior management and on boards of directors as well as having lower salaries, but they also see after four years of Labour government that the holders of power and their advisers are men.

There is talk of a backlash in the Labour party by men who feel they lost out to the number of women candidates at the election and now want their turn at the next election. So again women will be pushed out in politics as they have many many times before. Labour is in danger of maintaining a closed circle of men who share the same culture and values, who enjoy power and do not want to give it up. As Anna Coote wrote: 'A Third Way that is crafted by elite insiders, reflecting their priorities, is intellectually frail and politically vulnerable . . . women's politics are an integral part of modern social democracy – an asset, not a threat or diversion. And women's votes will remain volatile.'[22]

Leadership in business and politics is limited

Senior managers say they want leadership throughout but their actions, behaviours and the organizational structures tell a different story. Self-interest and positional power to use and abuse rose in the 1990s. In this environment leadership is stifled. Is this picture any different elsewhere in the world?

The Japanese picture of organizations

Japanese companies were considered good examples for the rest of the world during the early 1990s. Then in 1997, a director of Mitsubishi Motors was arrested on suspicion of paying off corporate racketeers. A couple of days earlier, three Mitsubishi officials were arrested suspected of paying Y9 million ($75 000) to corporate gangsters in exchange for guaranteeing not to disrupt shareholders' meetings with embarrassing disclosures between 1995 and 1997. Mitsubishi was not alone.

Police in Japan discovered at least ten leading companies were involved with a leader of the *sokaiya*, a racketeering organization, also arrested in the Mitsubishi scandal. Previously, in 1997, officials at seven Japanese companies mostly in the financial sector had been arrested for making pay-offs. The top management of four leading securities companies, a leading processor and a retailer, resigned as a result of *sokaiya* revelations, as did 60 executives in the financial sector.

Shareholder power

How did this happen and will corruption continue in Japanese business? For decades *sokaiya* bought shares in companies and then set about harassing the executives during the shareholders' meetings. At the peak of this activity in 1982, the *sokaiya* numbered nearly 6800. Legislation was brought in to address this situation and in June 2000 – after 80% of companies with a listing held their annual meetings – only about 400 *sokaiya* took part, according to Alexandra Harney of the *Financial Times*.[23]

The problem in Japan stemmed from the assumption that the economic growth they had experienced for several years would continue regardless of policy or people. The assumption was smashed for a while during the global crisis of the 1990s. This misguided belief was strongest in Japan where the entire ruling system was set up to avoid the necessity for any individual taking responsibility for anything. For years, politicians have known things were not working well, but no one was capable of making difficult decisions in the national interest. Japan's economic downturn occurred in slow motion, giving plenty of time for its leaders to bring about difficult but manageable changes. First the land prices crashed ten years ago; then stock prices; and then the entire banking system looked threatened. But the politicians and bureaucrats buried their heads in the sand and hoped the problems would go away. They did not, and when their neighbours began to crumble during the global crisis, Japan could only follow. Positional leadership without responsibility is dangerous.

Today, Japan's economy is growing strong again but still needs to properly address issues which include revamping the financial system and ditching regulations that coddle business. No one has broken the money links between inefficient industries and the ruling party. The global economic problem was a political problem but its propagation was the 'management mindset' of control without responsibility. This was reflected throughout the Far East, where the global financial crisis of the late 1990s began.

A global story

The story begins on 25 June 1997 when the new Finance Minister in Thailand, Thanong Bidaya, began to discover the true state of his country's foreign exchange reserves and the problems in its financial system. A handful of people in the central bank were in the picture but had been hiding the information from the Thai government and the public. Mr Thanong knew he would not get the relevant information by simply sitting in his office as his predecessor had done, so he drove to the bank and demanded the information from the governor of the Bank of Thailand, Rerngchai Marakanond. He found information that horrified him. Thailand's reported foreign reserves of over $30 billion were a myth and were in fact $1.14 billion, which was equal to two days of imports. But the full picture was to get worse.

The central bank's Financial Institutions Development Fund (FIDF) had lent over Bt200 billion ($8 billion) to struggling financial institutions. The country's largest, Finance One, had alone received over Bt35 billion from the fund in the first quarter of 1997. This lending had effectively drained seven years' worth of the Thai government's fiscal surpluses; the central bank was printing money to make up for the rest. The financial system was sucking out government money like a black hole, with no end in sight.

Within hours a leak began as influential brokers and privileged journalists were quietly told the FIDF would not be buying new shares in Finance One – even though it had promised to do so in a press release one month earlier. Two days later, Finance One shut down along with 15 other finance companies. Five days after that, Thailand was forced to free its currency from its long-standing peg to the US dollar, plunging East Asia into a financial turmoil.

A domino effect began as one by one Asian countries were affected. Following Thailand came Malaysia, then Singapore, Indonesia, Hong Kong, South Korea and then Japan. However, the repercussions started to fall out in the USA and Europe after South Korea. No one believed South Korea would be affected when the Asian crisis began. After Thailand's situation became known, the IMF had a list of who they thought were at risk which included Indonesia, Malaysia, the Philippines and even China. South Korea was not on the list.

Kim Young-sam became President of South Korea in early 1993 during a mild recession. He promised to boost growth by encouraging Korea's large conglomerates to invest heavily in new factories. Many of these were the *chaebol*, large family-run corporations such as Hyundai, Samsung and Daewoo. An investment-led boom followed but there was a cost to pay in the form of heavy debts and excess production capacity. Then in 1996, South Korea's largest export – computer memory chips – collapsed in a glutted global market. Cars, shipbuilding, steel and petrochemicals were also affected. Short-term foreign borrowing rose to try and cover long-term debts. The fuse was lit.

In January 1997, Hanbo Steel collapsed with $6 billion debts. How did this happen? The government had forced banks to lend to the company – an example of the phoney capitalism which was part of Korea. Political scandals followed and forced government changes. The new Finance Minister, Mr Kang, an advocate of the free market, allowed Korea's biggest speciality steelmaker to fall – the first to let market forces control. Kia Motors ran out of cash and asked for funding to prevent bankruptcy. It was refused but with elections looming and the banks refusing to lend any more money, the Finance Minister nationalized the carmaker. The slide accelerated and Korea tried to get support from the USA and Japan. This would avoid having to use the IMF and the strict conditions it would impose. The US Treasury refused.

The only option left was to deal with the IMF. This decision was made in November by the President and secret meetings began. Mr Kang, the Finance Minister, proposed to announce the request for an IMF rescue with two reform packages. The first would involve immediate new laws to improve the government's financial supervision, give independence to the central bank on monetary policy, and require consolidated accounts from the *chaebol*. The second would widen access to Korea's financial markets for foreign investors and ease trading limits on their currency, the won. However, parliament refused to pass the financial reform laws and Mr Kang was sacked.

Lim Chang-yuel, who had been the Trade and Industry Minister, took his place. Having served with the IMF, and with a reputation for tough negotiating, it was hoped he could get a better deal for Korea. A government fund of Won10 000 billion was established to liquidate bank loans, and the government promised to merge shaky financial institutions. This was in line with Mr Kang's plans except for one point: there was no request to the IMF. Of course it didn't work and Mr Lim had in the end to request a loan from the IMF. Negotiations began.

Meanwhile, the US foreign office were concerned that North Korea might try and take advantage of the situation and the USA had 37,000 troops in Korea. So in late November 1997, President Bill Clinton telephoned President Kim and outlined the situation and warned him that Korea would be 'severely punished' by the international financial community if a deal was not quickly reached. However, Mr Camdessus of the IMF refused to approve the deal on the table because of Korea's reluctance to close down insolvent financial institutions. Ironically, it was *Mrs* Camdessus who made the Korean officials think when she remarked to them over a luncheon she hosted: 'The one thing I learned from the medical profession [she had been a nurse] was that it was not only the medicine that counted, but the way that the patient takes it.'

A deal was signed that evening in early December for $55 billion. Yet the problems were still not over. Foreign bankers questioned South Korea's commitment to undertaking the IMF reforms. Some critics of the IMF argued that the conditions it was imposing were strict. The unpopular deal lost President Kim the election. He was replaced by Kim Dae-jung by a narrow margin, who now proposed a new financial package with the US, for despite the initial inflow of funds from the IMF deal, the financial market in South Korea was still falling and its foreign currency reserves would be exhausted by the end of December.

The new deal, known as 'IMF plus' which included the USA and other lenders to speed up payment of the next instalment of funds, was reluctantly agreed because of the worry of Japan being triggered next with a banking crisis. On Christmas Eve, Lim Chang-yuel, the Finance Minister, announced that the IMF and eight country lenders had agreed to advance $10 billion to Korea to prevent a debt default, and the US government and foreign banks decided to roll over loans to Korea. The so-called 'economic crisis' was far more than a matter of the free market and economics.

The Malaysian Prime Minister screamed: 'The free market has failed and failed disastrously.' But can you blame the free market when it was in the hands of bankers and politicians who hid the truth for so long?

Two years on Korea is changing its business structures which began with Daewoo whose name means 'Great Universe'. Chairman Kim Woo-choong started the company in 1967 with a $5,000 loan. It began as a textile business, importing raw materials and exporting finished goods. Nine years after setting up Daewoo, the government gave Kim Woo-choong a failing shipbuilding business and asked him to turn it around. His success led to further companies in need of rescuing. Each time the expansion was funded by loans until by the end of the 1970s Daewoo had nine times as much debt as equity.

Today Daewoo is involved in the manufacture of everything from ships to cars, while its construction unit builds houses, skyscrapers and shopping centres. Its securities business is Korea's largest brokerage. Now Daewoo is being dismantled into just six trading units, all connected to the automobile brand for which the group is best known. The remaining 20 or so will be floated off or sold. Daewoo Cars has just closed its dealerships in the UK showing that even the best of the group can tumble.

This break-up of the *chaebol* is perceived as central to the last part of re-engineering the economy in Korea. The President is leading a campaign to achieve this. The largest is Hyundai with 39 subsidiaries, which plans to split into five separate businesses by 2003. Samsung has 89 trading units. Their structures enable them to carry huge debt, which made them highly vulnerable during the crash. The concern for the government is that if the break-up of the *chaebol* leads to mass redundancies there will be political fall-out for the present administration.

Nearer home

After nearly a decade of breaking with the Communist stranglehold of the USSR, Russia has so far failed to create viable institutions of power. Under Yeltsin there had been an impression of a civilized state with a president, a federal parliament and private banks. The reality was he behaved more like a czar who lost control of his cabinet, the parliament and the people. He changed prime ministers as often as the weather changes but clung to power until the handover to Mr Putin.

In Russia today, except for the Communists, there are no real political parties so individuals are fighting for power, rather than putting into place the laws Russia needs. The pressure is tempting a return to a command economy. The more the present leaders fail in Russia, the more the people look for some outsider to come along and put things right.

'If only there was a woman we could vote for. The men have made quite enough of a mess in this country with their aggression, their drunkenness and their corruption. A woman could hardly do any worse. I would give her a chance.'[24] This came from a middle-aged Russian man and was reported in the *Independent*. It came days after Ella Pamfilova announced her campaign to stand for the presidency. Launching herself on International Women's Day she said 'We should not be thinking of reversing privatization, but in the process of market reform, we have not cared enough about human beings. This has led to national degradation and a sense of hopelessness.' She added: 'We must invest in job creation, education and science. If our social decline continues, no amount of military might will save us. Russia is a rich country and we simply do not have the right to live as poorly as we do now.'[25]

Ella Pamfilova knew she could not win but she continues to have influence. Mr Putin is adopting a 'father of the nation' approach which is proving popular. Leadership based on position and power has encouraged a helpless people as corruption rewards those who abuse their power. As an *Economist* columnist wrote: 'When the mighty fall, the mere mortals get scared.'[26] Pouring money into the region is not sufficient. Countries need to learn that individual responsibility and openness are more effective than control and deceit. But when control and deceit is all you've known, it is hard to change. A tight control is gaining ground today as the media have shown over Russia's involvement with Chechyia. Now responsibility lies with Putin. In a hierarchy it is easy to abstain from responsibility unless you are the positional leader.

Shunning responsibility

Absence of responsibility was a key factor in the 144-page damning report on the EU Commission in 1999.[27] Along with allegations of fraud, bad management and nepotism, it lists a devastating catalogue of lax management reaching up to the highest level. The worst part is the claim that the European Union's 14 000-member executive civil service is reluctant to take any responsibility for its actions. Here we have again leadership based on position without responsibility or accountability. The report's conclusion states 'The studies carried out by the committee have too often revealed a growing reluctance among the members of the hierarchy to acknowledge responsibility.'[28]

It continues: 'It is becoming difficult to find anyone who has even the slightest sense of responsibility. The temptation to deprive the concept of responsibility of all substance is a dangerous one. That concept is the ultimate manifestation of democracy.'[29] This is rather worrying when many of the 20 commissioners at the head of the organization are former politicians or ministers and even heads of government. The outcome was all 20 commissioners resigning, including Jacques Santer eventually.

We are not seeing leadership in the world

My conclusion is that what we are seeing over and over again whether in business or politics is not leadership. Individuals have reached the top of their hierarchies by being managers and continue to express management not leadership. Koch and Godden say: 'The vested interest of management and its power is clear.'[30]

Therefore, when individuals hear the comment that leadership is required throughout and training in leadership is necessary, three barriers appear. The first is that individuals want to express their own leadership, not what they are currently seeing. Second, leadership development through traditional training is very limited. Finally, when management dominates even the thinking in a business, it is impossible to have leadership expressed throughout. The question remains – do organizations really want leadership throughout, or only for a few? Management grips tightly to its vested interests and has seen the rise of the 'professional manager' in the last 20 years.

The past and present emphasis on management and management development including MBAs has stifled leadership throughout society and is reflected in our organizations on a global scale. The solution to the vested interests of which we have seen examples in this chapter has been to put in place rules and policies to deal with the corruption. The aim in doing so is to try and make it more difficult for individuals without asking why this has happened and why management as a system in its own right has replaced leadership.

Rules and more rules

For example, in the UK new rules have been incorporated in national politics with an 'ethics committee'. MPs have to state their earnings outside their role as an MP. These rules have had to be extended to the House of Lords because some individuals were exploiting the gap. In other words the rules make it more difficult for corruption to take place but they do not address why it happens.

Likewise, there are plans for an ethics watchdog to uncover corruption and malpractice across all the EU institutions. This includes the European Parliament where abuse of expenses remains widespread. Resistance to the proposals are immense and it is feared that the proposals will be watered down when the powerful staff unions in Brussels have finished. Self-interest and personal gain is rife in the management of these hierarchical structures of business and politics where management rules over leadership. Where else does the self-interest of managers push out leadership? In recent times there have been some surprising revelations uncovered.

Buying decision-makers

The abuse of management position and pursuit of personal gain has penetrated the world of sport where leadership has been weakened. The International Olympic Committee has been shown to be susceptible to 'handouts'. One past committee member who resigned in 1991 over his own charges of conflict of interest described the present situation as a culture that has stopped concentrating on the needs of the athletes and devoted itself to the members' creature comforts.

On investigating how bids were won it appears individual cities were approached by agents offering to buy them votes. Salt Lake City, which will host the Winter Olympics in 2002, is one of these. Initially it was alleged that an education fund was set up whereby the relations of six IOC members were awarded scholarships worth £250 000. More recently, it has been claimed that a health care fund was set up providing relatives of members with free plastic surgery and even a knee replacement. The Manchester Committee claim that one IOC member asked for a reimbursement of £12 000 apparently stolen from his room but he refused to report it to the police.

Another member claimed reimbursement for an air fare already paid for by the IOC.

In New York, Senator Mitchell said that the credibility of the IOC had been 'gravely damaged' by the Salt Lake City episode and by 'a broader culture of improper gift-giving'. He added, 'Ethical governance has not kept pace with the paid expansion of the Olympic movement . . . the IOC's lack of accountability has directly contributed to the gift-giving culture.'[31]

Have we bred a generation of managers whose self-interest was propagated during the 1980s politics of individualism and greed? Is this why everywhere is crying out for leadership that has a moral connotation that appears to be lacking in management? In which case training leaders in the same way as we train managers has to change. Leaders have to replace managers, which will be difficult to accomplish when these managers guard their positions, even in the world of sport.

Commercial opportunities

Football in the UK has recently seen directors of clubs behave in questionable ways. Newcastle United fans forced the resignation of disgraced directors Douglas Hall and Fred Shepherd. But when they forced their way back onto the board it resulted in the resignation of Denis Cassidy, the chairman of five months. It would seem that when big media organizations like BSkyB are offering large sums of money for clubs, directors of clubs want to be in on the action and will push others out.

When the government rejected the takeover of Manchester United for £623 million by BSkyB it came as a relief to many fans and supporters. The reaction from the Independent Manchester United Supporters' Association was that Martin Edwards, the chief executive of the club, should resign. Spokesperson Ray Eckersley explained that his position was untenable, his treatment of the fans as purely for his own commercial interests meant that he had to go. When the fans challenged the deal, Edwards and other board members called them rabble-rousers. Leadership is non-existent in some football clubs where abuse of position and self-interest has put the sport into disrepute. This environment has resulted in poor behaviour on the pitches as well as among fans.

Outdated attitudes

One way of maintaining power and control is to support outdated beliefs and attitudes. Inside the football world itself outdated sexism is being challenged. Football agent Rachel Anderson won a discrimination case when she was ejected from a dinner by the Professional Footballers Association. Tony Banks, Graham Kelly and David Davies all refused to attend the male-only function. It was the deputy chief executive Brendan Batson who personally asked her to leave.

More recently Vanessa Hardwick, one of the country's most qualified female coaches, won a tribunal after being refused an advanced licence even though she gained higher scores on the course than men who were granted the licence. At her tribunal Ted Copeland, then manager of the England women's team, remarked that women were too emotional because of 'their menstrual problems'.[32]

After winning her case the tribunal ordered the FA to grant her the advanced qualification within 28 days or pay a further settlement. It also recommended that future assessors of the advanced licence by given equal opportunities training. However, the FA chose not to give Vanessa the licence and paid the additional money. She has now gone to the USA to work where football coaching doesn't suffer the same problems. The end result will be women's football in the USA dominating at world-class level and the UK missing out on the opportunity because of the mindset of a few. A few misusing their position can do a great deal of damage.

House of storms

One of the established bodies in London that has received much criticism is the Royal Opera House. In 1997, a House of Commons report on the Royal Opera House concluded that 'the current board should dissolve itself, and the Chief Executive should resign, with immediate effect.'[33] What had led to this public damning? News that their £78 million National Lottery grant had been used to fund redundancy payments and that Sir Jeremy Isaacs, the previous chief executive, had received £10 000 a month for almost a year after he left did not help. The parliamentary committee were not the first to reach their conclusions.

The Arts Council had tried to keep a rein on its highest-funded client which received £15 million a year from them. In 1992, after having examined the Royal Opera, the Royal Ballet and the Birmingham Royal Ballet, Baroness Warnock was asked to head an appraisal team to review the organization as a whole. On completion, Lady Warnock pointed to 'an inadequacy of management, both executive and non-executive . . . Personnel management is inadequate and the overall general management is in need of considerable improvement . . . The tendency has been to decide what is right artistically first and to count the cost later.'[34] Lady Warnock said that the situation was so serious that the building development plan should be cancelled or postponed.

They come and go

In May 1997, chief executive Genista McIntosh resigned after only four months and the organization was barely saved from insolvency by a £2 million loan from two 'friends'. In the same month, the Royal Opera House embarked on rebuilding its home at a cost of £214 million of which £78.5 million came from lottery funding. Mary Allen took over as chief executive after running the Arts Council. Both she and her chairman Lord Chadlington were heavily criticized in the parliamentary report. 'Given her experience of public office,' the report concluded, 'Ms Allen's conduct fell seriously below the standards to be expected of the principal officer of a public body, whose loyalty should first and foremost be to the organization which employs her . . . Lord Chadlington should have appointed a new finance director with greater urgency, instead of permitting nearly a year to elapse.'[35] Even past boards were criticized: 'The failures of the board in 1995 are responsible in considerable measure for the House's current crisis.'[36]

So chief executives and board members have come and gone, but the problems remain the same. Why can't the Royal Opera House resolve its problems which have gone on for a very long time? The main answer is the collective 'culture' of the board where external interventions were not welcome. An arrogant management mindset was the main problem. Michael Kaiser, a New Yorker who turned around the fortunes of the American Ballet Theatre, is holding the reigns. But problems remain with stops and starts and he too has announced that he is leaving. Can one person change the 'management mindset'? An embedded culture – one that is not flexible – is a serious challenge in any organization.

Incompetence and racism

The publicized Lawrence case left the Metropolitan Police in disarray in 1999. The conclusion of the Lawrence Report was that the investigation had been fundamentally flawed and 'marred by a combination of professional incompetence, institutional racism and a failure of leadership by senior officers.'[37] The present structure and culture makes it very difficult for leadership to be expressed. For those who are good at management, the hierarchy has rewarded them well. Although the Lawrence case has brought into the public arena the way the police handle their work, it is only one of many cases where the police have failed the public they 'serve'.

Another case began late one night in January 1997, when Michael Menson was found on fire on a north London street, his clothes reduced to ashes, his body a mass of burns. In the early stages of the case, the police proceeded on the basis that Michael's burns had been self-inflicted. Therefore no investigation was required. By the time he died two weeks later as a result of his injuries, the police had still not taken a statement from him.

Change in the force will be difficult because its management mindset is so entrenched in its culture. It can be likened to that of a sleeping industrial giant that has not noticed seismic changes in the marketplace. Therefore, trainees and police officers can go on the best training programme – but when they return to the workplace and are told to keep their heads down and are bullied by senior officers, nothing will change.

Public opinion of the police has declined as stories abound such as the payout awarded to 14 officers who were involved with the Hillsborough disaster – which many believe happened through police incompetence in the first place. The figure they received was £1.2 million – a figure which dwarfs the amounts paid to the families who actually lost children. Also, if an officer takes early retirement on the grounds of stress or other injuries, they receive enhanced pensions and compensation which cost the service nearly £100 million in 1998. A further £20 million was awarded for injuries in 1998.

Corruption by the few

Corruption has always been an issue for the few such as Elmore Davies. When he was detective chief inspector he sold information he had on drug investigations to criminals. On one occasion, not only did he take £10 000 but also the information led to another officer being intimidated before a trial that included threats to his children. Members of the police hierarchy state that this sort of corruption is extremely rare although those same senior officers attended a meeting in June 1998 where they agreed that corrupt officers existed throughout the UK. One director of intelligence stated that police corruption had become pervasive. These activities include theft of property and drugs during searches, planting of drugs or stolen property on individuals, supplying details of operations to criminals, and aborting investigations or destroying evidence.

It is usually the Metropolitan Police that is seen as the 'bad apple' and Sir Paul Condon has openly said that he might have 250 corrupt officers working for him. But the Met should not be made the scapegoat. In

1992, Sir James Sharples the Chief Constable for Merseyside became aware that some of his officers were selling important information on police operations to drug dealers, such as the identity of undercover informers and the date and time of proposed arrests. Then a joint operation by customs and the regional squad obtained the itemized phone records of a number of known drug dealers that showed that these criminals were telephoning numbers inside both Merseyside police drugs and fraud squads.

In 1995, customs officers provided further evidence that Merseyside police officers were still selling information to drug barons, which sabotaged operations. At this point Sir James Sharples gave permission to customs officers to tap the telephones. After the investigation, Sir James Sharples quietly disbanded the drug squad, fraud squad and serious crime squad. An unknown number of officers retired early on grounds of ill health or were moved to less sensitive positions. Sir James went on to set up an anti-corruption force called the 'Professional Standards Unit'.

Something seriously wrong

All this shows is that something is very wrong in the police force as a whole where a mindset of self-interest and abuse of position is allowed to exist. Added to which, when something comes to the surface, the officers are allowed to retire. It is very difficult if not impossible for leadership to exist in this environment. In 1999, 15 of the 43 forces could not find full-time assistant chief constables and had to readvertize their vacancies as the quality of those applying was below standard.

During 2000 the 'Corruption Prevention Strategy' was sent to all forces informing them that anyone giving information on other officers will be offered new identities and relocated to safe houses. It recommends telephone hotlines for those brave enough to speak out and suggests a national campaign using the National Crime Squad and the National Criminal Intelligence Service. The police chiefs involved with the report are concerned about the way officers 'close ranks' and become silent when something surfaces. Therefore they say: 'As a result of cultural pressures, there have been cases when an individual has openly made a report, where this has been seen by peers as an act of treachery and disloyalty.'[38] This explains why, when speaking on a leadership programme for the Metropolitan Police I asked whether they trusted their colleagues, the reply was overwhelmingly 'No'. In this environment how can leadership be encouraged to be expressed?

In the US one of the problems has been heavy-handed officers in the LA Police Department. There are cases of robbers being shot dead with claims that the officers were shot at first – only to discover that the dead men were not carrying a weapon. In 1999, two promising, highly decorated officers were convicted of armed robbery and drug dealing. In an effort to reduce the sentence, one came clean on police corruption in the force and the information left many reeling. He admitted handcuffing an unarmed 19-year-old with no police record, and then with his partner shot him at point-blank range. This situation is rare but possible when the hierarchy encourages abuse of position and lack of responsibility.

Can you see how difficult it is to develop leadership in organizations? This isn't just a problem for those with a poor reputation. The cracks are showing in the most unexpected places as the breakdown of hierarchies continues.

Arrogance rules

Most people would not expect to find abuse of position and lack of leadership in the medical profession. However, the need for change and the public outcry at bad doctors has led some to try to modernize the royal colleges that run the service, in order to make doctors more accountable. Fundamental to this is competence. Once doctors have passed their exams no one until now could question their competence. But public scandals such as those involving children at Bristol, the UK cervical screening disasters and finally the Harold Shipman trial have enforced change. Resisting this are the royal colleges who see it as taking control away. The 'management mindset' is rife here too.

The British Medical Association were also angry when private medical insurer Bupa announced that one quarter of the 80 000 hysterectomies performed on women in the UK each year were not necessary. Now Bupa have said that any gynaecologist wishing to perform such an operation has to comply with a list of reasons. Doctors at the BMA are outraged as they see this as an insult to their clinical freedom. However, the government have launched a new body, the National Institute for Clinical Excellence, to look into the practice of medicine. The new body has already received hostility from some doctors who feel their independence being threatened.

More recently the doctors have taken action themselves by voting for reforms of the General Medical Council at the annual BMA conference. The doctors voted four to one on having no confidence in the GMC and said it should begin urgent reform of its structures and functions.

Harrassment

The legal system cannot escape either, although a few law firms are realizing the benefits of developing teams. Leadership research carried out in 1999 found that discrimination and harrassment of young solicitors had doubled in two years.[39] Further, every case cited was said to be an example of a frequent occurrence and one in ten of those trainee solicitors claimed that the behaviour took place on a daily basis. At the same time, the Law Society has found that qualified female solicitors are paid around £13 000 less than a male colleague of equal qualifications and experience. All this at a time when leading lawyers in the City of London are earning salaries approaching £1 million according to Legal Week.[40]

The Crown Prosecution Service lawyers and police were severely criticized in February 2000 by a judge for incompetence following the collapse of a drug trial that included an allegedly corrupt detective. The trial was abandoned after the prosecution failed to disclose hundreds of pages of evidence to defence lawyers. Our organizations are failing the people they purport to serve.

Culture of intimidation

The prison service has also been criticized for lack of leadership and replaced with management that is incompetent. Wandsworth in particular was found to have a culture of intimidation and racism by some of the prison officers according to the chief inspector of prisons in 1999.[41]

Perhaps one of the worst findings of how the 'management mindset' operates was in the inquiry into the personality disorder unit of Ashworth Special Hospital. The report, which has two volumes, is highly critical of the Special Hospitals Service Authority, the former body overseeing Ashworth.[42] Charles Kaye, who was the authority's chief executive, is singled out for failing to intervene when he knew there were problems and for not keeping the health department informed. In addition, the hospital's chairman, Paul Lever, resigned from his post pleading pressure of work. The report concludes: 'The hospital's negative, defensive and blame-ridden culture is so deeply ingrained that we doubt if even the most talented management team could turn it around.'[43] In other words, *management cannot resolve the situation.*

Today the solution being implemented is to break up these large institutions into smaller units where it is hoped improvements can be made.

The growth of the manager

In every aspect of life that we have looked at here there has been a decline in trust, responsibility and leadership. Instead there has been a growth of managers and management control eminating from self-interest. How have we developed these managers? Do we need more management development?

In 1947 in the UK, a national scheme for colleges led to the Diploma in Management Studies and the growth of management colleges beginning with Henley followed by Ashridge. But it was the Frankes Report[44] in 1963 which led to the establishment of the

London and Manchester Business Schools in 1965. In 1969 the Mant Report[45] found only 7% to 8% of British managers attended courses lasting one week and that most of those attending were 'fast-track' managers. Course design was a misnomer because it wasn't understood what managers actually did. In 1970, the Owen Report[46] showed that most organizations were doubtful about the value of post-graduate training and criticized the business schools. There was a gap between academics and the business world in seeing what was needed to develop managers.

Severe recessions followed in 1974–5 and 1980–2 with training cut to a minimum. In 1985, Coopers and Lybrand were commissioned by the Manpower Services Commission to investigate training (in which I was involved). The report, 'A Challenge to Complacency', showed widespread ignorance of training at board level.[47] The report showed that in many cases training was not seen as an important contributor to competitiveness or profitability but rather as an overhead to be cut when profits were under pressure.

In 1986, the University of Bath found that over half of all UK companies, including some of the largest, made no formal provision for management training.[48] Of those who did, the median expenditure was less than £600 a year for each manager. Finally, also released in 1986 were the reports by Handy, and Constable and McCormick.[49] Charles Handy investigated management education and training in the USA, Germany, France and Japan; while John Constable and Roger McCormick examined the UK situation. From these it was clear that the UK was lagging behind and it was concluded that Britain must do more to develop its managers.

Action from organizations

This time, instead of the government intervening, the corporate world took action along with the Foundation for Management Education, the CBI and the British Institute of Management. Charles Handy proposed a charter setting out a code of good practice and in 1988 the

Charter Group was formed under the auspices of the new Council for Management Education. Since then, management training has had a successful decade. To some extent, management rather than leadership was emphasized because it lends itself to being taught and is necessary to keep hierarchical structures running.

Today, the emphasis on management has been institutionalized into corporate cultures and Koch and Godden go as far as to argue that managers have become a 'class' in their own right.[50] The question we need to ask is: having had a series of initiatives and action to develop management in the last 50 years has management development and training improved how organizations run? In addition, would yet another initiative and further bodies change the present situation? We need to try and answer these questions before finishing the chapter.

Management today

The issue for managers today is that of order and control. So it was at the birth of management during the Industrial Revolution. Keeping control in the large organization becomes a primary concern – control of costs and control of resources. Managers spend more and more time looking inwardly, attending meetings and dealing with inward issues. A survey by Booz-Allen[51] and Hamilton found that only 20% of senior executives' time was spent on external, non-organizational matters, and of that only 5% or less was on direct customer contact. This means that 80% of senior managers' work is spent sorting out internal organizational matters. The picture today is as John Kotter describes, organizations are 'over-managed and under-led'.[52]

Restructuring and more government initiatives will not resolve things. Yet we keep on trying. Now England, Northern Ireland, Scotland and Wales each have a 'Council for Management' still trying to improve the standard of management in the UK. When will the realization dawn – that hierarchies and with them management do not have a place in the future.

A whole paradigm shift is required and the longer this takes, the more stress and struggle there will be. As Koch and Godden believe: 'It is perfectly clear that the intellectual foundations of the managed corporation have already collapsed. Its legitimacy and rationale will soon be under terminal attack.'[53]

In *Liberation Management* Tom Peters wrote: 'Middle management, as we have known it since the railroads invented it right after the Civil War, is dead.'[54] Yet Peters' ideal organization – customer-driven, led by visionary individuals with small, flexible teams – is still confined to comparatively few companies, which tend to be in the service or 'knowledge' industries.

Management as a power base has proved tenacious in organizations preserving their power and self-interest, as we have seen. It is also costing those organizations millions without adding any value as time is taken up on internal issues. Koch and Godden argue that management not only takes an increasing share of corporate wealth but also adds complexity to decision-making and internal processes and has precious little to do with the customer.

A different world

Today we find the world is more interconnected and more complex than we ever imagined it to be. It is no longer the place for large hierarchies with managers who are no more productive than when Henry Mintzberg studied them in 1973, when he found most of their time was spent on firefighting and being interrupted. In fact I believe that the more management there is, the greater the problem and the more difficult it is to change.

The world began a transformation toward the end of the twentieth century. Technology enables management to be bypassed but many organizations have yet to seize this opportunity. The new era is not just technological – the technology is a driving force for something even greater. We are on the cusp of an age where the way we see the world will be very different – so different that our thinking will completely change. It will effect how we work, our personal lives, the way we treat other life, our education and even our religious beliefs. As Birchall and Lyons say: 'The where and when of doing work is rooted in the distant past of the Industrial Revolution.'[55]

Today the world is changing fast and has no room for the past to still be present. Workers now are very different from those who filled the factories in the Industrial Revolution. Today's important issues are quality, responsiveness, globalization, outsourcing, partnering, teams, sustainability, diversity, social and environmental responsibility and above all *leadership*.

The failure of many

The problems and issues shown in this chapter are just different facets of one single crisis. They derive from the fact that most organizations subscribe to an outdated world view of organizations and the people who work in them. This perception, which is linked to the whole ethos of management and its subsequent behaviour, is inadequate for dealing with a world rife with chaos. At the same time many of the business, public and political 'leaders' at the top fail to see how these different problems are interrelated. They also fail to see that the present solutions will not help future generations because their management mindset has not changed. Even in the universities, structures and processes are management and many academics have failed to see and change their thinking.

The civil servants advising politicians also tend to have the old management mindset and the departments contain individuals with 'old thinking' who are used to 'playing safe'. For example, when I was part of a task group to explore the issue of improving management in the UK it quickly became apparent to me that the decision had already been made on the solution; that leadership wouldn't be included because it was 'too much of a hot potato' according to one of the senior civil servants; and a typical play safe initiative was launched. Why do we keep trying the same solutions over and over again? The real hypocrisy is that the department has now launched an 'academy of leadership' for their own people to attend.

Finding the way forward

There *are* solutions to all the major problems of our time – but they need a radical shift in our thinking, values and world view. It is going to take courage – and lots of it – to stop doing things the way we always have. We must instead burn our bridges and create the conditions, structures and thinking to move forward, with no return.

Vaclav Havel addressed an audience at Independence Hall in 1994, stating:

> There are good reasons for suggesting the modern age has ended. Many things indicate that we are going through a transitional period, when it seems that something is on the way out and something else is painfully being born. It is as if something were crumbling, decaying and exhausting itself, while something else, still indistinct, were arising from the rubble.[56]

The evidence of decay has been shown here. The focus now must be on the real transformation needed for the future. Our task is to identify what the new organizations will be and how they will enable individuals throughout to express and practise their leadership. This is a new stretch of road which hasn't been driven down before. For the journey we need a compass rather than a map. The place we want to achieve we know – how to unleash leaders throughout organizations. Just as previous pioneers had no map, there is no map for us here as this is new territory but a compass will give us some direction.

Our knowledge and intuition, used correctly together, become the wisdom and compass to guide us. Laura Berman Fortgang says: 'Wisdom is the memory of the soul.'[57] We need to use all the experience, memory and learning we already have to help us as well as the courage to walk into the unknown. It may involve being uncomfortable or thinking the unthinkable. Therefore before we begin our new journey we need to look back to ensure we take with us all possible knowledge. For in our heads lie the answers as they always have before. The task is to unlock them.

4

The Time Traveller

*There should be somewhere in the works some kind of a principle
that uxles only make wuxles, and never vice versa, and so the
world is turning from uxley character to wuxley character all the
time and this one-way business of the interactions of things should
be the thing that makes the whole phenomena of the world seem to
go one way.*

Richard Feynman, *The Distinction of Past and Future*

It was at the Futures Conference that I met the elderly gentleman
who was dressed rather strangely but had a kind face. His conversation demonstrated an intelligence that was remarkable while also
naively enthusiastic. His name was Herbert – Herbert George Wells. I
explained that I was at the conference to pick up the thinking on the
future but that I also wanted to study the past to gain a wisdom that
could be shared with readers to help them understand what we need to
leave behind to build organizations that enrich human potential and
with it leadership throughout.

Surprisingly Herbert offered to help. 'Come with me. I have just the
thing and I would enjoy the ride too.' Following close behind – which
wasn't easy because he walked so fast – we left the conference building
and approached a narrow lane that was blocked by a large covered object.
Pulling the cover off, Herbert said: 'Get inside quickly and we will soon

get the information you need.' Needless to say I followed his instructions but with concern as to what I was getting into. He called it his time machine – TM for short. He said, 'If I can be HG. then this is TM.'

I needn't have worried. Herbert helped me find the information I needed. I will share with you the information I found out and see where it takes us.

The evolution of organizations

Retrospection in search of information that will help us to move forward means not just looking back into a hundred years of history or even a thousand years. To really understand why we build organizations the way we do, we need to begin in prehistory, which is before written history. The journey back in time seemed to take several hours in TM.

As a race of human beings we have more prehistory than history and we carry this within us in our subconscious. In other words, we are still influenced by the whole of our past, not just a part of it. As we explore our past, we can see how much we still carry with us today and thus take into our organizations. Although there are limitations on what we can learn from the distant past as our world view has changed, there are patterns which if identified can help in the learning process.

The German philosopher Hegel believed that although we cannot learn from history, through reflection we acquire new thoughts that were not available to the participants at the time. Our present organizations are struggling with a different world. What can the past world show us that will help in the future?

Organizations require some form of civilization. Until recently it was believed that civilization began with the Egyptians 3000 to 5000 years ago but we now have evidence of much earlier civilization. In fact the further back in time we go, the more we are discovering that our perception of prehistory is invalid. The strongest example of this is our perception of Neanderthal Man.

Experts have found that Neanderthals had larger brains than us but this does not mean they were more intelligent. There has long been a debate over whether they could talk or just grunt. This was partially answered by the discovery at Mount Carmel of a 60 000-year-old hyoid bone. The hyoid bone lies at the back of the tongue and is unattached to any other bone. Thus the discovery showed that Neanderthals were physically capable of speech.

Recently Jele Atema, a flute-playing professor of biology at Boston University, has made a working copy of a 50 000-year-old Neanderthal instrument and concluded that it was more than a simple flute. He claims the instrument is a recorder or 'fipple flute'. This shows a sophisticated technology to make a tone-producing mechanism.

To dispel the 'myths' of Neanderthal there is evidence that these prehumans took care of the deformed and injured and even had the ability to successfully perform amputations, which requires a basic level of medical knowledge. When one of their community died there is evidence that they buried the dead. One burial in Shanida found a 60 000-year-old man whose grave contained the remains of seven flowering plants. At first this was perceived as a floral offering as we lay wreaths today. However, the flowers were found to have medical properties still used as folk remedies in that part of the world.

Even earlier, Homo sapiens buried their dead as we've found in Israel. Therefore, communities were laying the foundations for civilizations and with them organizations much earlier than we tend to acknowledge and certainly much earlier than the once-believed 5000-years-ago timeline depicted with the Egyptian civilization; for our early ancestors were building communities, developing culture in the form of expected behaviour, laying down rules and organizing their work and lives.

In 1998 two archaeologists Francesco d'Errico and April Nowell made a discovery which has resulted in a split in our present understanding of the past. They found a sculpture from the Golan Heights more than 200 000 years old, which challenges our views of the intellectual abilities of our early ancestors. This explodes the current belief that modern thinking humans began 50 000 years ago with sudden activity in art through cave paintings in Europe.

Indeed in the spring of 2000 two British archaeologists found evidence of humans producing art 350 000 to 400 000 years ago. The evidence from the Bristol academics was found in the African region normally associated with the birth of Homo sapiens. It suggests that the Stone Age inhabitants were producing painted art before they evolved into our species.

A new understanding is developing which sees mankind's intellectual capacity evolving very slowly over the past 2 000 000 to 400 000 years. In fact, other archaeologists are also now finding artefacts much earlier than 50 000 years old all over Africa and the Middle East. A new paradigm is emerging about our past and with it discoveries of civilizations older than we have previously accepted.

Early civilizations

Archaeologists have found the remains of a remarkable culture that existed in Turkey between 7000 and 5500 BC. They estimate that the town had a population of around 10 000 people. Living like this there must have been some means of social organization and consensus. Like other cultures it evolved from earlier beginnings.

In Malta and Gozo there are remains of temples built before and around the time of the First Dynasty of ancient Egypt. However, where Egypt is unique is that it built the first nation state and organizations took their place. The state of Egypt embodied the spiritual beliefs and aspirations of a people in a theocracy. State, religion and culture were one. The country relied on the dictatorship of the kings and queens and this varied. If there is any doubt in the minds of anyone about whether leadership is only bestowed to the few chosen ones, they need only look at the differences of leadership in the pharaohs to prove that leadership is an individual gift to every human being.

We are now going to explore three different civilizations that influenced how we build our organizations today. Much of history has been written about men whereas here we are going to look at both men and women in these civilizations as they had different roles in organizational life. This is because to unleash leadership everywhere it is important to recognize that women's history has been different to men's and this has had an influence on the story of organizational life.

The Egyptians

Egypt was the product not only of human ingenuity but of racial grouping influenced by the River Nile and the land. The Egyptians did not regard themselves as a chosen people; they were just people and accepted others who adopted their culture wholeheartedly. We have to shut out the pictures of the movies to really understand these civilizations.

From the end of the fourth millennium BC, the progress of this nation was rapid. The River Nile provided water for drinking, cooking, washing and waste disposal in an otherwise arid part of North Africa. The river also provided a major transport route linking the towns and cities from south to north. However, what was unique about the river was its annual inundation or flooding, which had a profound effect on the development of Egyptian civilization.

Every year from July to October, heavy rain in Ethiopia caused the river level to rise dramatically, flooding, irrigating and cleaning low-lying land and depositing a deep layer of fertile mud that was rich in minerals. Settlements built on higher ground were protected by dykes. When the water retreated in late October it left thick moist soil for crop cultivation, providing a rich harvest in late spring. The land was able to dry under the hot sun which also killed many agricultural pests. This provided a stable environment where little changed.

Throughout thousands of years Egypt retained a pyramid-shaped society. At the top of the hierarchy was the king, queen or pharaoh who was also acknowledged as semi-divine. As such they were head of the priesthood, the army and bureaucracy. A long way below them came the upper classes, privileged families probably related to the pharaoh. These few assisted in the government of the country by functioning as high priests, generals and senior civil servants, receiving large estates as payment for their work.

Further down came the educated middle classes who, being literate, were able to join the bureaucracy as scribes and accountants. Below them were the lower middle classes, semi-literate and illiterate artisans who worked as joiners, potters, sculptors or artists. The largest layer of society included soldiers, servants and the peasants who worked the land owned by the pharaoh, private landlords or the religious foundations. Slaves, who were never very numerous, did not form an independent social class and this is worth noting. In Greek and Roman civilizations slaves were an important part of daily life and a factor in their downfall. In Egypt, the majority of people had a role to play and work to carry out.

The second feature to note is that although it was difficult to move up or advance in the class structure because of the education method, girls had more freedom than other civilizations. Each father taught his son his particular craft and daughters were restricted by their biology. However, they did have a freedom which surprised Greek scholars who studied Egypt.

The freedom of women

When Europeans who studied Egypt found images of women in prominent or powerful roles, they dismissed the findings as 'ritualistic'. The truth is that women were legally independent citizens who exercised varying degrees of self-determination. The Greeks were shocked by this and when the Greek historian Herodotus visited Egypt at the end of its dynastic period he was intrigued to find women who appeared to be as free as their menfolk.

Egyptian women married and had children but were also seen labouring in the fields or alongside men for public works. Both male and female servants cleaned houses and did the baking – but the laundry was done by professional washermen. For the upper class, the men worked outside the home and the women tended to stay indoors, giving them a paler appearance. For others, women were paid for the work they did; they could own, buy and sell their own property, make wills and choose which of their children would inherit.

Many women help religious posts and many held titles of 'governor', 'judge', 'overseer of doctors' and even 'vizier', the highest administrative rank below king. The monarch was usually male, but women occupied the throne on at least five occasions. The one most remembered was of course Cleopatra VII but the reign of a far greater female pharaoh produced a growth in art, culture and exploration as well as stability not unlike that of Elizabeth I of England.

Hatchepsut ruled over an age of internal peace, foreign exploration, prosperity and architectural achievements. Like Elizabeth she had to appear as a man at times. 'I know I have the body of a weak and feeble woman, but I have the heart and stomach of a king, and of a king of England too' (Queen Elizabeth I at Tilbury before the Armada).[1] Hatchepsut had to take this even further and is depicted as male as well as female in wall carvings where she is dressed in men's clothes and even wearing a false beard. For both, being a leader required them to express their 'maleness'.

After Hatchepsut's death there was a serious attempt to destroy her memory but it failed. Some believe her achievements would have been more greatly regarded had she been a man and perhaps this is why she portrayed herself as a man. Yet when you see the tall standing obelisk of Hatchepsut at the Temple of Amen at Karnak or the three-tiered temple Djeser-Djeseru you cannot ignore the pharaoh behind them. Her words are written for all to remember: 'My command stands firm like the mountains, and the sun's disk shines and spreads rays over the titulary of my august person, and my falcon rises high above the kingly banner unto all eternity.'[2]

However, the lives of the majority of Egyptian women remained uneducated and they only carried out domestic skills. This freedom wasn't the freedom we know today in parts of the western world but compared to the Greek women it was a huge step toward equality. The relevance of Egyptian women to us now is that their role in organizations was nearer to that of women in our last century than to that in other ancient civilizations. It could even be argued that their lives were similar to women in the 1950s before the contraceptive pill. If Egyptian society had continued, would women's history have told a different story? Would our organizations and leadership have had a different history with a stronger influence from women? What we do know is that whether women or men, in Egypt life evolved around religion and beliefs.

A strong religious culture

It is difficult for us to understand the gigantic pyramids as a product of religious fervour, rather than royal egomania conscripting a servile multitude. The people did not regard the funeral works as a whim but as important to everyone. If the king passed safely into eternity as a god, then the immortal status of the entire people serving him in the next world as in this would be guaranteed. In this sense Egypt was a collec-tivist society. As such, organizations were structured and processed to fulfil the needs of this status quo which lasted longer than any other civilization since. It is startling to realize just how little the fundamental core of Egyptian society changed in its long history. The same stability is apparent when looking at the daily lives of the ordinary people.

The craftmanship was of highest standard. The trained stonemasons were organized on military lines divided into named troops. These skilled men were kept on permanent duty and both they and their families were provided with ample supplies of food, clothes, housing and other necessities by the State. The unskilled labour that supplemented them during the flood season was also fed and clothed and probably grateful for the work during this part of the year.

Throughout the third millennium and for most of the second BC, Egypt was great. Surviving two internal breakdowns, a foreign occupa-tion and maintaining the matrix of its religion, culture and political system with remarkable continuity was an achievement. When collapse happened it came from the desire of people to act out their own thoughts and opinions. They no longer believed they were part of the collective. The idea of individual conscience emerged. Therefore, unlike our society which has seen 100 years of gradual emancipation change the lives of everyone, for the Egyptians the change was from seeing themselves as a collective conscience to one of the individual – whether male or female. However, this individual conscience was limited.

During the second millennium BC Egyptians secured for themselves individual rights in eternity but not on earth. Their attachment to *maat*, the principle of order, hierarchy and submission, inhibited them. They were not only disciplined from above, they imposed on themselves a self-discipline which no culture can indefinitely survive. Their fear and hatred of disorder and of the anarchy they believed lay within their own personalities killed their own creative spirit. We see this in managers today. The Egyptian people's refusal to admit their own individuality as human beings on Earth and only in the afterlife resulted in an independent state becoming a helpless colony with no leadership.

The strong hierarchy and reliance on a king-god pharaoh suppressed their leadership gifts. Throughout her history, Egypt retained an inflexible, pyramid society. No one questioned the uneven distribution of wealth and status or the inherited right to rule. These were regarded as necessary to maintain the status quo. The gifts of leadership were only expressed by those at the top of the hierarchy – for the rest it was suppressed by their thinking and need for order.

Lessons

What should we learn from this? The longest civilization maintained its stability through the perception of being part of a collective order that relied on a king-god pharaoh to rule with a structured hierarchy to maintain order. In return people felt they had security in their lives. Leadership was the right of those on top of the hierarchy and therefore based on position. The internal collapse came about when the people realized that after death they could express themselves as individuals and be leaders in their own right.

Now think of your father and grandfather who also lived and worked in a hierarchical order which they accepted in return for stability provided by governments and employer. Leadership was based on position. During the 1980s downsizing on a massive scale resulted in people realizing that security as they had known it was no longer available. At the same time more people were being educated and technology opened up access to information not experienced before. The rise of the knowledge worker began and with it an individual consciousness is emerging. However, this time it is available now, not after we are dead. This transformation is in its early stages but has implications for leadership.

Are we depending too much on the person at the top of the hierarchy? Is the huge stress in organizations today caused by individuals desperately needing to express their individuality, creativity and leadership rather than compliance?

What we can learn from the developments of Ancient Egypt is very relevant today. *The hierarchy works when there is stability and order. When people want security above freedom of the human spirit they will comply.*

Today we live in a world of fast, constant change. People want to express their creativity and leadership. People want to have more control over their own lives and resent even governments telling them what to do and eat. They are taking up issues politics and succeeding rather than taking these issues to existing organizations or political parties to deal with on their behalf. People have lost faith in hierarchies and prefer direct action. People want to express their individual leadership while hierarchies are trying to use more control through performance measures and targets. We are sitting on the edge of a time when breaking away from control and order will occur. But there remain those who are still clinging to order and control and those who are responding by building even bigger hierarchies. Like the Egyptians, their time is coming to an end. Their world changed with the rise of another civilization – one where organizations were different based on a different set of beliefs.

Greek civilization

The civilization which has influenced the west more than any other was that of the Greeks. The term 'Greek' or 'Greece' tends to refer to Classical Greece between around 500 and 300 BC. This was not a single society but it was a single culture. It began 1000 years earlier with the forming of the first cities.

A city (*polis*) was an autonomous political community of people inhabiting a particular territory that included both rural zones with villages and (but not always) a more developed zone that can be called a town. In Athens a set of beliefs, attitudes and mindset was generated, which shaped the organizations in this culture.

Whereas in Egypt religious organization was a dominant factor in the society, in Greece it was political organization. The two main forms of political organization evolved by the Greeks were those of a people (*ethnos*) and of a city (*polis*).

The Greeks had expanded through emigration in the Mediterranean. Wherever they went the land was already inhabited by peoples who had been there a long time, speaking non-Greek languages and with civilizations of their own. Whereas the Egyptians would welcome people who accepted their way of life, Greeks always regarded outsiders as less than themselves and therefore not entitled to become 'Greek'. This way of thinking influenced western Europe for 2000 years as its countries invaded others.

Back in Athens new institutions were adopted during the first 40 years of the fifth century BC, giving the *demos* (citizens) more weight in the constitution of Athens. It is sometimes said that this is where democracy began, and has influenced democracy in the world until quite recently. For the Athenian *demos* did not comprise of the whole of the population of Athens. Democracy was not for everyone.

There were no professional divisions with regard to access to political power. However, throughout the classical period people were divided into four census classes according to the amount of real estate they owned. The *demos* excluded women, foreigners and slaves. It also excluded proved cowards at war, prostitutes, city debtors, those who mistreated their parents, traitors, conspirators and the authors of proposals for laws that ran contrary to the constitution. It was an intolerant democracy and very hierarchical.

A 'citizen' was a male born from a citizen father who had reached the age of 18. Then in 451 BC a law restricted the criteria for citizenship. To be a citizen a male had to have both a citizen father and a mother who was the daughter of a citizen. Athenian citizenship was closed for anyone outside and participation in political power was jealously guarded. Therefore fifth-century democracy in Athens was characterized by a strict system of exclusion. The limits of this institutional democracy were of an economic, social and ideological nature and political power remained in the hands of a small number of citizens who were members of a section of Athenian families. This model of democracy has been copied in much of the world in the evolution of democracy as we know it today. Can a society have democracy and slaves? Aristotle and Plato believed so.

Slaves in a democracy

Slaves were very much a part of life in Greek civilization. The most common form of slavery was rural servitude. An entire rural population was often deprived of its liberty and would work on the land of the citizen landlords. In the cities, chattel slavery developed. These slaves were bought and sold in markets like any other chattels. A slave was a living instrument and had no rights at all and was legally deprived of any personality. His master had total power over him and could beat or even kill him if he chose. Having slaves was justified to the Greeks.

Aristotle wrote:

Some thinkers hold that . . . for one man to be another's master is . . . unjust, for it is based on force . . . Property is part of a household . . . for without the necessities even life, as well as the good life, is impossible . . . so the manager of a household must have his tools, and of tools some are lifeless and others living . . . and a slave is a live article of property . . . If every tool could perform its own work when ordered, or by seeing what to do in advance . . . masters would have no need of slaves . . . Therefore all men that differ as widely as the soul does from the body and the human being from the lower animal (and this is the condition of those whose function is the use of the body and from whom this is the best forthcoming) – these are by nature slaves . . . and for these slavery is an institution both expedient and just.[3]

Aristotle

Aristotle (384–322 BC) was one of the most profound figures in Greece and his influence is strong in western life today. Born in the north of the region he spent most of his life as a resident alien of Athens. His works touch every branch of knowledge except mathematics. Aristotle was primarily a scientist, an enquirer into nature, rather than a philosopher in our sense. In particular he was a biologist and zoologist as he studied nature which was derived from studying animals and plants, as opposed to humans.

Aristotle believed that every living thing had its *telos* or end. For example, an acorn will become an oak tree, but this did not mean 'eventual' or 'finished' but rather 'complete' in the sense of 'perfect'. On Aristotle's animal-to-human spectrum humans occupy 'the most complete' or perfected end. This completion for Aristotle is not just of form but of essence. This also included gender. Male humans were the most perfectly masculine of all living things, female humans the most feminine. However, he believed women were both opposite and inferior to men.

This 'arrogance' of putting men at the top of the living hierarchy was reinforced through Greek stories and myths. It has justified the suppression of women's leadership for 2000 years. But we will see later in the book that keeping women out of the hierarchical structures of power for so long is today an advantage as our generation of women who are having to look at new ways of working.

Women in Greek society

Stories in a culture are strongly held and transferred from one generation to the next. The ancient stories of the gods include the creation of Pandora, the first woman who thereafter labelled women as a 'beautiful evil'. This justified the role of men controlling women in a civilization. Women were subjected to the authority of their master who would be their father, then husband and perhaps brother. Women had no legal identity and could not inherit land. The majority of girls received no education. This could be regarded as surprising as the god of wisdom was Athena who was female. In Greek society only a few could express leadership through political organizations in a hierarchical world.

Work and organizations

The Greeks even had a hierarchy of occupations, which began at the top with the ownership of land, agriculture and in particular the cultivation of cereals. Craftsmanship and trade were depreciated because they did not bring those who practised them independence since they had to sell what they produced. In addition, these skills did not develop the physical qualities of the citizen but instead caused atrophy. The judgement passed on the work of the craftsmen had nothing to do with its economic importance to the city, but to its relation to political activity. Manual work was not despised but with slavery, labour was depreciated.

The education system

Basic education began at the age of seven and lasted for 14 years. Primary education focused on reading, writing and counting. At secondary school, physical training was considered very important. Higher education, which Plato believed should continue until the age of 50, took the form of 'continuous training'. Here you can see the influence of the Greeks on the western world still today.

Administration takes control

Just as large organizations today use managers to administer them, something similar happened at the time known as the Hellenistic period following the Classic Greek period. The area the Greeks had conquered in the Mediterranean was huge and time was spent settling the 'kingdoms'. The idea of a divine king became attractive. The Hellenistic kings ruled in their regions. As soon as politics stopped being a rational attempt to make citizens themselves responsible for public affairs, and instead turned into submission to the force embodied in a single man, it once again became natural to conflate the sovereignty of kings with that of the gods.

After years of gradual progress, Athens had given itself a regime placed under the protection of law but powerless to ensure the survival of the city and its freedom. Kings were strong and protected by law but cities were weak. The Hellenistic monarchies introduced 'administration' and bureaucracy took hold. The Greeks had never adopted their expertise in lifestyles and organization to the continental empire. Alexander, now ruler, decided to administer the occupied lands using administration methods. Administration and bureaucracy needs stability and time for decisions and actions. This worked for a while but disillusionment was creeping in.

A spiritual gap

Despite the progress made by Greek science and philosophy, a spiritual gap was appearing in society. The 'gods' had disappointed many for they repeatedly failed to ward off disasters. As well as the disappointment from the gods, there was a feeling that political institutions had also let the society down. Mistrust of those in politics grew.

During the Hellenistic period a new aspect was introduced into the religious domain – one that involved setting oneself at a distance from politics and society. Commenting on the Greeks, Jean-Pierre Vernant wrote: 'For the experience of a truly internal dimension to take shape, there had first to have been the discovery of a mysterious and supernatural power within man himself, the *daimon*-soul.'[4] The word *daimon* already existed in Homer but since Socrates, the 'daimonic' had been understood as a breath that communicated dynamism to an individual, a sort of immanent source of inspiration. Is this the 'dynamic urge' Robert Fritz[5] speaks of, or the 'self-actualization' that Maslow[6] wrote about? Whatever we call it, the requirement is to look within ourselves to acknowledge it.

The Greeks had found within themselves a reality not encountered before – a religion of the soul. It didn't involve rejecting the past beliefs, but rather encouraged individuals to take a new look at themselves in a way not previously known. The power that had always been feared in the outside world had led to cults and rituals, but now that power was present within themselves. This individual energy was inside human beings. The soul appeared increasingly as a new dimension; one that it was important to liberate by turning away from the constraints imposed from outside. Once again, as with the Egyptians, an individual conscience came into being. Today this is occurring in our organizations again where there is a rise in acknowledging 'the human spirit' in the workplace. Since the Industrial Revolution spirit has been suppressed.

For the Greeks, wars and the threat from Rome loomed. Running their large domain they had to constantly fight against aggressors in order to have peace and liberty. The Greeks were forced to fight in their world – to be masters and free or be beaten and become slaves. In the end the power of Rome expanded into the Greek world.

Today, organizations are having to fight to survive by focusing on cutting costs more and more to remain the masters. They are fighting against an inevitable transformation.

Lessons

The lessons from the Greeks are:

- Self-interest of the few 'fat cats' will not be tolerated forever.
- People will realize their own power and turn away from the constraints of large organizations.

Many individuals are already leaving the corporate world and setting up different ways of working. In the UK over 500 000 people will set up in business during the year 2000. This will continue as the younger generation of managers wants to spend more time with families. A different set of values are becoming the desire of many, alongside their deeper disenchantment of big business. Back in Greece a new civilization was threatening, and organizations would evolve again.

Roman civilization

On Palatine Hill on 21 April in the year 753 BC tradition asserts that Romulus founded the city of Rome. The 'Roman people' were a more heterogeneous body than the *demos* of a Greek *polis*. The people did not wish to rule the Roman state, but wanted to be able to protect themselves against the abuse of power from those who did rule it. Rome was not the work of one man but of many, over many centuries. It was shaped through the long struggle between the patrician aristocracy and the rest.

Private life was centred on the family together with the slaves or freemen who lived with them. The position of women was quite complicated. Legally a woman did not exist in her own right, but Roman women found ways around the legal disabilities, especially as wives. From the third century onward, the commonest form of marriage bond was one which allowed the woman control of her own property after the age of 25 and divorce was easy should things not work out. A Roman marriage could be very much a partnership of equals. However, a woman could not vote or sit on a jury – and it was unthinkable for her to take part in politics. The Romans were astonished to find sovereign queens such as Cleopatra or Boudicca.

Work

In a large city there was a variety of craftsmen and traders. Rome was an agricultural centre, so farming tools and instruments were needed to be made. A few professions became established, notably the architect, lawyer and schoolmaster. Doctors were few and not highly skilled.

Over time, the political institutions of Rome were transformed from those of a city state to a world empire. Cultural change was rapid and a new Graeco-Roman civilization came into being. If there was a capital of the world, it was Alexandria in Egypt with its harbours attracting trade. It was here the three civilizations met. Egypt was now run by a Greek, Ptolomy, and Rome wanted to possess it for its empire. The story of Cleopatra, Julius Caesar and Mark Anthony is history. But the story of Rome continued and with it a new form of administration.

Administration and the civil service

Once established, Augustus set up a great political administration which lasted over 100 years. Claudius gave it further reforms to strengthen and rationalize the civil service. Four bureaux were formed: one for laws; one for finance; one for records and archives and one for judicial matters. Each was run by a freeman and under Claudius these individuals of Greek descent ruled, dominating more than their departments. These individuals enriched themselves with huge fortunes and were hated by the Senate.

Today we can see that the foundations of Europe were influenced by Roman civilization, and that the administration in Brussels for the European Union should learn the lessons of the past.

Slave labour

The importation of slave labour on a large scale to Italy and Sicily was an enormous social disaster for Rome. Many people lived with families and spent time with the children of those families. Quietly they were influencing the thinking of the people. It has been estimated that 250 000 prisoners of war were brought in as slaves in the first 50 years of the second century BC and thousands of others would have come through commercial channels. It was another hierarchical society with slaves at the bottom and a few at the top with all the power.

The Roman Senate and power

The great families were dominant in the Senate and held a near monopoly of the highest offices of the State. When it came to elections, advantage was to those with the standing and money to build up the most powerful political machine. This is similar to American politics today. Roman nobility followed convention rather than ideals, one of which was a hostility to the concentration of power in the hands of an individual for too long, as Caesar learned.

Eventually a military autocracy took control with endless military coups d'état until Diocletian, followed by Constantine who restored and reformed the Republic. Constantine became more and more convinced that power lay with the God of the Christians and that God favoured him. Rome's alliance with Christianity brought a new dimension into its life and for many the world empire stopped here. To regard the early Christians as the good ones and the rest bad is an oversimplification often shown in films

Lesser known is the story of Hypatia, born in Alexandria around 355 AD to Greek parents. Alexandria had always been a place for learning and Hypatia was brilliant at mathematics and astronomy. Her teaching and private lectures led to fame and she became an adviser on current issues. Hypatia was regarded as having courage, veracity, civic devotion and intelligence. Around 390 AD, Christianity became the official religion of Alexandria but Hypatia did not convert. She became a threat to the Christian patriarch Cyril. In 415 AD a group of monks pulled her from her chariot and into a church where she was killed most horribly. Hypatia was a threat to those who wanted to control people's thinking and lives. There are still places in the world where a similar challenge to a religion would not be tolerated.

The Roman Empire was riddled with people battling for power. Control and power were fundamental. A weak military and severe taxes all contributed to its downfall. Yet there are lessons here again for us today.

Lessons

The lesson which stands out from Roman civilization is: *the elite in the political administration can easily become a huge financial burden with individuals filling their pockets and using power to influence.* In Brussels and Strasburg today this lesson is again being learned as it is in other parts of the world.

Lessons from our history

When we study civilizations of thousands of years ago we find they are still with us today in how we build and run organizations. Even further back in time, our ancestors still influence us. How is this possible? Is it that we are still fundamentally the same as then? Or is it that we just don't learn? Or could the reason be that we need to change our thinking? Why do we still build pyramids today and put in place huge bureaucracies with managers to run them? How did our modern organizations emerge?

5

Shaping Modern Organizations

*You travelled a great distance to get here. The dream of your life
has been dreamed from eternity.*

John O'Donohue

History of the modern managed organization

The birthplace of modern industry began in the eighteenth century
when much of the economic activity in Europe was owned by the state,
guilds and family businesses. The Quaker families such as Rowntrees and
Cadburys are names we still recognize today. By the nineteenth century
the scale of these enterprises had expanded but they were still family-
run. At this time a small number of 'professional' firms emerged and also
began to expand. These included lawyers, bankers, estate managers,
engineers, stockbrokers and accountants.

By the end of the nineteenth century, another type of organization
had emerged – the managed business. These were owned by shareholders and run by 'managers'. These organizations developed through
changes that were to have long-lasting effects. The first was the idea of
limited liability which emerged in the US and UK during the 1800s.
First in New York in 1811 a standard corporate charter was established
so that if the companies failed the owners could keep their wealth. It

was in 1844 that the English Stock Act followed. This led to invest-ment from the landed aristocracy and gentry in the UK. These individuals, mainly in England, owned the majority of the country's wealth but slowly realized that the future was in industry, the railways and canals. Investment gave them an opportunity to increase their wealth further.

The third change was the growth and formulization of stock exchanges. Now as well as trading shares in privately owned companies, quoted companies became popular where shareholders were anonymous. The gap between ownership and management became greater. By the twentieth century the majority of industrial and commercial organiza-tions ceased to be family-run.

From the Second World War to the end of the twentieth century, organizations run by professional managers and owned by share-holders became the dominant norm. During this time another devel-opment helped their growth: the expansion of international trade and operations creating multinational corporations who could use mass advertising.

Meanwhile, public sector organizations grew and followed the corporations in scientific management practices. Universities provided MBAs for both the private and public sectors, providing 'fast-track' executives who could scale the ladders in their hierarchies.

Today we live in a world of fast, constant change where hierarchies are not able to deal with a different world. People want to express their creativity and leadership but feel constrained in the present structures that remain from the past.

Abraham Maslow asked:

> Why is it that we often design organizations as if people naturally shirk responsibility, do only what is required, resist learning, and can't be trusted to do the right thing? Yet most of us would argue that we believe in the potential of people and that people are our most important organizational assets. If that is the case, then why do we frequently design organizations to satisfy our needs for control and not to maximize the contributions of people? . . . For centuries human nature has been sold short.[1]

So why do we still build hierarchical organizations? With that question on my mind I thanked Herbert for the ride into the past.

'Did you find what you wanted to know?' he asked

'Yes,' I replied, 'but I'm left with more questions and I wonder if I will find the answers.'

Herbert looked me straight in the eye. 'You will if you now explore the discoveries and ideas that were coming out of the twentieth century.'

We said our goodbyes and I thanked him before he stepped into his machine alone. I walked away, wondering if I'd ever see him again. Herbert was right; the answers are here.

Why do we build hierarchical organizations?

The common answer to the question 'why do we build hierarchical organizations?' is – there is no other way. The search to find the true answer led me to scientist and writer Richard Dawkins who introduces the concept of 'memes' in his book *The Selfish Gene*. He explains that just as genes transport characteristics from one body to another, memes transport human culture from one body to another.

Dawkins says: 'Just as genes propogate themselves in the gene pool by leaping from body to body via sperms or eggs, so memes propogate themselves in the meme pool by leaping from brain to brain via a process which, in the broad sense, can be called *imitation*.[2] This is done through ideas, songs, articles, fashion, ways of making things, doing things and seeing the world.

Genes are instructions for making proteins, stored in the cells of the body and passed on in reproduction. The competition of genes drives the evolution of the biological world. Memes, on the other hand, are instructions for carrying out behaviour, stored in brains and passed on by imitation. Their competition drives the evolution of the mind. The two are very different.

Dawkins writes: 'The computers in which memes live are human brains . . . If a meme is to dominate the attention of a human brain, it must do so at the expense of "rival" memes.'[3] Therefore, in order for people to believe in one god, other gods had to disappear. Yet memes are not easy to dismantle. Aristotle is long gone, but his memes are still around. Seeing the world as a hierarchical order with human beings at the top, superior to all other living things, pervades our society. Long-term selfish interests keep memes alive. But Hawkins believes we can rebel against them. He adds: 'We are built as gene machines and cultured as meme machines, but we have the power to turn against our creators. We, alone on earth, can rebel against the tyranny of the selfish replicators.'[4]

Memes come to us from parents, teachers, friends, bosses, colleagues, books, films, television, newspapers and so on. Taken together, they become our culture and we believe that how we do things is how everyone else should do things. When we invade another culture, we believe our way is right and that others should copy us. Civilizations have acted on this time and time again.

To show how strong these memes are let me explain how they destroyed a civilization through its own inhabitants, where the invaders were just the catalyst. One of the founders of the Inca civilization saw in the night skies that at a certain time in history their world would end. This meme was told in songs and stories and known to all Incas over generations. At the time when the sky was almost at the prophe-sied point, Spanish soldiers invaded the land. In just days thousands of Incas were slaughtered – by a handful of Spanish with little resistance. The people were living out the meme. Thus is shown the power of these units of information in our collective consciousness, which carries their views across out minds.

Today we build our organizations in the same way as Egyptian structured pyramids; we set up administration and public organizations as the Romans did. In these organizations we place 'managers' to run them. At the top are so-called 'leaders'. Today these ruling people are not pharaohs or divine monarchs but they still need stability to rule.

This meme of how organizations should be structured and run needs to be challenged for, as we've seen, it doesn't work in a world of flux or where people want to express their potential, creativity and leadership.

New issues and constant changes are overwhelming our organizations and the processes we have developed for them. Such ways are based on beliefs that include:

- companies will make profits year after year after year after year;
- putting people in prisons will curb crime;
- shelter will get rid of the homeless; and
- the care system will take care of the young.

Many organizations in the public sector are not working and no amount of money will make them work as they are presently structured and containing the present thinking. Large companies can only cut expenditure more and more until there will be no more to spare. The crisis is everywhere, whether expressed in political, ecological, economic, race, social or health terms – and our response is to continue to do more of the same.

Does an answer to the present situation lie in memes? Through understanding memes we may be able to break away from trying to think and act in ways that don't suit the present and future. Through understanding memes we may be able to move towards finding a way that transforms organizations to unleash the leadership potential within them.

Understanding memes

Whereas genes travel vertically down generations, memes travel both vertically and horizontally. Like genes they are selected against others in the available pool. This results in groups or mutually compatible memes, known as memecomplexes, found cohabiting in individual brains. Memes like other memes that compliment themselves. From this process they become powerful. The meme for believing organizations should be hierarchical is likely to cohabit with the memes that believe in power based on position, paying those at the top substantially more and justifying this. This meme then becomes powerful because memes spread themselves without regard to whether they are useful or positively harmless to us. They are totally indiscriminate.

Where do new memes come from? They come about through variation and combination of old memes. In the human mind we mix up ideas and turn them on their head to produce new combinations. We have seen this in scientific paradigms. We also know that when memes are strong they prevent us from seeing beyond them. For example, many believe the only structure for organizations is hierarchical. Another example is given by Dawkins himself who admitted that biologists had so deeply assimilated the idea of genetic evolution that they tended to forget that it is only one of many possible kinds of evolution.

In archaeology as in science, the same process has occurred to limit what individuals 'discover'. But now individuals are creating new memes and the whole belief system of our history is being questioned as the new memes spread. The same challenge must occur in organizational and human development.

Millions of memes are competing for space in our brains. Which memes are more likely to end up with a home and be passed on to others? The answer is the memes that make up a memecomplex. These are groups of memes that come together for mutual advantage. Once in a memecomplex they form a self-organizing, self-protecting structure that welcomes other compatible memes and repels other memes. Can you now begin to see why change is so difficult in organizations when you are dealing with these complex replicators in the heads of individuals?

In addition, when memes become part of a person's self-concept they become connected to who that person believes themself to be. For me to change my memes means changing myself. This powerful process can be seen across society in individuals who believe they are superior to others because of class, race, gender or even role or position in a hierarchy. We do not even have to like or agree with the memes we pass on but to only engage with them through statements such as 'I like . . .', 'I hate . . .'

Finally, to show the power of these little replicators let's look at how people react when organizational change threatens their possessions such as car-parking space, size and make of car or business expenses. Animals have possessions; for example, a robin owning a territory which he guards or a lioness owning her kill. Human possessions can likewise enhance personal status and provide a genetic advantage. However, our possessions attach themselves personally to 'I', not just to the body it inhabits.

Our relationship with possessions is different from animal behaviour. Our possessions define us, whether they are a house, a car, paintings or books. You become not just a living creature but all these things as well. Memes protect themselves by becoming who you are. If transforming an organization threatens the memes, watch how individuals behave. The memes will try and protect themselves by repelling new memes that do not enhance the present ones. Thus organizational development is such a huge challenge. Hence restructuring has changed little and 'leadership throughout' remains two words.

The present memecomplex is holding us back. The only way to bring about real transformation is to replace it with a new one which is better for everyone – employers, employees, customers, public servants, society and so on. This new set of memes will need to be part of the new paradigm for the twenty-first century, and strong enough to become a memecomplex with a large number of individuals. The next chapter will show the new memecomplex that is emerging in the world. From here we will learn how to truly transform organizations to unleash leaders everywhere.

6

The Paradigm for Change

To think differently – this thought must enter deeply into our intentions, actions and so on – our whole being.

David Bohm

*J*t is clear from the previous chapters that something is wrong with most organizations today. If we look at the problems – the self-interest of individuals, the desire for control and order, the inability to resolve issues, a stressed and dissociated workforce – it becomes clear that these problems and issues are not a shopping list but rather are linked together. These systemic issues are all related to leaving an 'old world' behind that includes our perception of work, organizations and human beings.

Our present limiting beliefs are influencing how we create and build organizations, how they should be run and who should benefit from them. We now know that through memes we are carrying thinking and culture that belongs to the past. This past goes back thousands of years. We also know that in order to change we need new memes. Here we will focus on what those new memes are.

To transform our organizations to enable leadership to thrive we need to acquire a radical shift in our thinking, our understanding, our values and our culture as organized human beings. This is known as a 'paradigm shift', a term first coined by Thomas Kuhn who described it as 'a constellation of concepts, values, techniques and so on, shared by a [scientific] community'.[1]

Capra expands Kuhn's definition to one we shall use here which he describes as 'a constellation of concepts, values, perceptions and practices shared by a community which forms a particular vision of reality that is the basis of the way the community organizes itself'.[2]

What this means is that we are shifting from the paradigm of a mechanistic world, where we see the human body as a machine, and life as a competitive struggle where individuals feel isolated and apart from nature, a world hell-bent on unlimited material progress through economic expansion requiring more and more, a world where the male is superior and dominant. Replacing the old world view is one which sees all life as connected to the natural environment, a holistic world rather than a world of separate, isolated objects and a world that values all living life. These new memes are waiting for us to spread them in the world. Today we have the technology to make this easier.

The new paradigm must now apply to organizations throughout society. We need a new way of thinking and a holistic model capable of transforming all organizations. This chapter will show the new thinking emerging in the world that will be the basis for such a framework.

Maslow wrote:

> As I tried thinking about these matters it quickly became very clear that pure theory of theories must at once be involved. For instance, that what we have here necessarily is a kind of holistic thinking or organismic thinking, in which everything is related to everything else and in which what we have is not like a chain of causes and effects, but rather resembles a spider web or geodesic dome in which every part is related to every other part in which the best way to see everything is to consider the whole darn thing one big unit.[3]

What is this 'whole darn thing' made up of? What is the 'one big unit'? The truth is we have been moving towards finding it during the last 100 years. During the twentieth century developments in different fields of learning have been taking us toward this new paradigm and understanding. The journey has not been a slow, steady progression, but rather has seen revolutions, backlashes, pendulum swings and oscillations. During this time these revolutions have appeared isolated, pure fluke and random. Yet they form a complex, organized wave – taking us to a new shore. They include quantum physics, chaos theory, systems thinking and ecology. This new knowledge together shows us the new thinking, the new memes needed to truly transform organizations and unleash leaders in the twenty-first century.

The quantum contribution

Before quantum physics the world view had been based on the notion of solid indestructible particles moving in a void. It was Einstein who, having associated the gravitational field with the geometry of space, then brought quantum theory and relativity theory together to describe the force fields of subatomic particles.

Today the distinction between particles and the space surrounding them isn't as sharp. In fact, modern physics shows us that material objects are not distinct entities, but rather are linked to their environment and that their properties can only be understood in terms of their interaction with the rest of the world. This interrelationship is crucial in our understanding of the world in the twenty-first century.

Through Einstein's general theory of relativity a revolutionary change of human perception of reality emerged. For atoms turned out not to be solid particles but rather vast regions of space in which extremely small particles – electrons – moved around a nucleus. It was also found that atoms have a dual nature – sometimes they are seen as particles, sometimes as waves.

This view of reality was very different to Newton's physics where the world consisted of tiny, discrete particles that bump into, attract and repel each other. These particles were solid and separate, each occupying its own place in space and time. In Newton's world, reality was determined, fixed and measurable. This orderliness made possible the Industrial Revolution that followed.

Quantum physics describes matter that does not exist with certainty at definite places, but rather has 'tendencies to exist'. In quantum theory you do not have things, but interconnections. Particles come into being and are observed only in relationship to something else. One of the pioneers in quantum physics was Heisenberg who remarked: 'The world thus appears as a complicated tissue of events, in which connections of different kinds alternate or overlap or combine and thereby determine the texture of the whole.'[4]

Here, nature is not isolated building blocks, but rather a complex web of relationships between the various parts of a unified whole. Our world isn't a machine-like entity, determined and fixed, but is one of interconnections and interrelationships. Yet we build organizations in fixed structures controlled by 'managers'. Even when we 'restructure', the fixed structures and processes remain. We are still seeing organizations in the 'old' paradigm. The memes are strong.

In classical mechanics the properties and behaviour of the parts determine those of the whole; the situation is reversed in quantum mechanics – the whole determines the behaviour of the parts. Can we say that the whole hierarchical organization determines the behaviour of the parts? I believe so. The structure of the organization limits individuals and the greatest of these limitations are seen in the expression of leadership and creativity.

The new paradigm perceives reality as a network of relationships rather than functional silos and hierarchies. Fundamental to this is the requirement to include in the new paradigm an understanding of the process of knowing. This goes beyond learning or analytical data, but taps into an intuitive knowledge. In a world of fast-pacing change this knowledge is vital. We have to trust our inner wisdom – our intuition. When we study scientific revolutions we find intuition rather than rigorous process is the driving force of individuals. The quantum world has changed our perception of a fixed, predictable world.

The systems contribution

Another twentieth-century development was systems. Systems thinking developed in several disciplines during the first half of the twentieth century. Paul Weiss took systems concepts to life sciences from engineering. Biologists pioneered the ideas with their view of living organisms as integrated wholes. The ideas were taken further by gestalt psychology and the new science of ecology.

The main thrust of systems thinking is to realize that the properties of the parts are not intrinsic, but understood only within the context of the whole. Thinking in simple building blocks is not sufficient; relationships have to be taken into account. In fact, systems thinking is contextual rather than analytical. It is also called 'holistic'.

One of its pioneers was German biologist Ludwig von Bertalanffy who wrote: 'In one way or another, we are forced to deal with complexities, with "wholes" or "systems", in all fields of knowledge.'[5]

Marilyn Ferguson sums up the theory when she says:

[It] sees all nature – including human behaviour – as interconnected. According to General Systems Theory, nothing can be understood in isolation but must be seen as part of a system . . . . Science has always tried to understand nature by breaking things into their parts. Now it is overwhelmingly clear *wholes cannot be understood by analysis* . . . In relationship there is novelty, creativity, richer complexity. Whether we are talking about chemical reactions or human societies, molecules or international treaties, there are qualities that cannot be predicted by looking at the components.[6]

Systems thinking became part of several disciplines that resulted in a unified approach to problems. This systems theory was named 'cybernetics' by Norbet Wiener. Those involved were not biologists but mathematicians, political scientists, engineers and neuroscientists. Their work led to the concepts of 'feedback' and 'self-regulation'. One of the important aspects of the cyberneticists' studies of feedback loops was the recognition that they depict patterns of organization. What cybernetics did for systems thinking was to distinguish the *pattern* of organization of a system from its physical *structure*. Structure is substance or building blocks. You have to ask: what is this made of? You measure or weigh it. Pattern is form or relationships. You cannot weigh or measure it – it is mapped. You have to make a configuration of the relationships. The difference between structure and pattern is crucial to the theory of living systems. It is also crucial to the transformation of organizations in the twenty-first century.

Systems thinking is the search for what Gregory Bateson called 'the pattern that connects'. In the twenty-first century, humanity is becoming increasingly connected by information. Through this we can see the apparent contradiction in the involuntary movement towards a global consciousness and the singular attempts at nationalism and 'holy wars' as the last responses of an old state of mind. Behind this people fear losing a sense of place and identity or of being controlled by some larger bloc. A systems approach can deal with this: one can be connected intimately with one's immediate region, but see that as part of a global whole. I am Welsh; I am British; I am European; I am from Planet Earth; I am a child of the Universe. As such I regard all human beings as part of one family. Now with technology I can communicate with them too. Yet much of technology is still being perceived and treated in old thinking.

Today, progress is perceived as technological innovation. However, it is necessary to balance this with the increase in human well-being. This one-sided approach to technology as machines for 'machines' is causing stress and it is based on old thinking. The use of computers is based on a world view of seeing human beings as information processors. This view is tied to the old paradigm of mechanistic knowledge and communication. The factories of heavy machinery have been replaced with offices full of computers focusing on the processing of information. Yet information does not create ideas; rather ideas create information. We have to move away from the notion of the workplace as mechanistic to a place full of human creativity, leadership, knowledge and spirit where humans connect with other humans. Information and technology will then take a more dynamic and positive role. Systems thinking focuses on seeing the whole and the relationships, both of which are fundamental in organizations.

Chaos theory contribution

The story of chaos theory is well documented by James Gleick in his book *Chaos*. In it he quotes a physicist as saying: 'Relativity eliminated the Newtonian illusion of absolute space and time; quantum theory eliminated the Newtonian dream of a controllable measurement process; and chaos eliminates the Laplacian fantasy of deterministic predictability.'[7]

In classical science an assumption is made that our universe has order and laws of nature that we just need to identify. Many of these laws we learned at school. From this scientists focused on finding order. Disorder was ignored or discarded. In the 1970s a few mathematicians, physicists, biologists and chemists began to find a way through disorder and irregularity. The interest has grown, and now that scientists are looking, they are finding chaos everywhere around us.

Chaotic systems are characterized by extreme sensitivity to initial conditions. Over a period of time, minute changes will lead to large-scale consequences. In chaos theory this is known as the 'butterfly effect', based on the widely known story of a butterfly that stirs the air today in Beijing causing a hurricane in New York next month.

As in other scientific revolutions the pioneers had difficulty convincing their colleagues and scientific bodies. Gleick says that those turning to chaos early on had stories to tell of discouragement and even hostility. One described the task facing them: 'Here was one coin with two sides. Here was order, with randomness emerging, and then one step further was randomness with its own underlying order.'[8]

Similar stories have also been told in personal accounts of the quantum discoveries made through Heisenburg and Bohr. What keeps individuals going when around them the world appears to tip itself upside down? In the story of chaos theory one commented: 'The glue that held us together was a long-range vision.'[9] This is something we must remember in transforming our organizations too for the new memes will be challenged by reactions ranging from scepticism to pure hostility. Our vision must be to see individuals everywhere able to express their leadership to enable the world to be improved for everyone.

Before chaos theory the expectation was that simple systems behaved in simple ways, while complex systems behaved in complex ways. In reality it has been found that simple systems give rise to complex behaviour and complex systems give rise to simple behaviour. Further, the laws of complexity hold universally, caring not for the details of a system's constituent atoms.

In organizations we assume a large corporation will be more complex than a small business. This assumption is used often as an excuse for not changing. 'It's easy for them to change, they are only a small business' is commonly used already. Today, this excuse will no longer hold weight as chaos theory shows another view.

Another issue that affects our way of understanding organizations relates to the decline of companies that is perceived as 'natural'. Gleick talks of the second law of thermodynamics and chaos:

Any process that converts energy from one form to another must lose some as heat, perfect efficiency is impossible. The universe is a one way street. *Entropy must always increase in the universe and in any hypothetical isolated system within it.* However expressed, the Second Law is a rule from which there seems no appeal. In thermodynamics that is true. But the Second Law has had a life of its own in intellectual realms far removed from science, taking the blame for disintegration of societies, economic decay, the breakdown of manners, and many other variations of the decadent theme. These secondary metaphorical incarnations of the Second Law now seem especially misguided. In our world, complexity flourishes, and those looking to science for a general understanding of nature's habits will be better served by the laws of chaos.[10]

Organizations do not have to decline and cut cost after cost to survive in a globally competitive world. The answer lies elsewhere and by taking on board the 'new thinking' shown here we will find that answer. Organizations are not isolated units. They have to interrelate with customers, suppliers, contract workers and so on. Therefore we need to understand how this works in the twenty-first century, and chaos theory can help us.

The ecological contribution

Another late-twentieth-century phenomenon is the growth of interest in ecology. The word 'ecology' was first used by German biologist Ernst Haeckel in 1866. He defined it as 'the science of relations between the organism and the surrounding outer world'.[11] Ecology added to systems thinking and introduced two new concepts – 'community' and 'network'.

The contribution of systems thinking and ecology is that they ask different questions to 'normal' science. Through the questions ecology has found that life is not about hierarchies but about networks within other networks. It is here that we can find a fresh view of organizations and their transformation if we realize that the organizations we work in can also be perceived as living entities.

This was explained in Arie de Geus's *The Living Company*. He wrote: 'All companies exhibit the behaviour and certain characteristics of living entities.'[12] He added that the idea of a living company had enormous implications for managers and for the bottom line of a company, but that too many managers ignored this, which was tragic. So what can we learn from those who study living organisms?

Chilean neuroscientist Humberto Maturana has spent his life asking deep questions about living systems. These have led him to two conclusions. The first is that the circular organization of the nervous system is the basic organization of all living systems; and the components that specify the circular organization must also be produced and maintained by it. He concluded that this network pattern, in which the function of each component is to help, produce and transform other components while maintaining the overall circularity of the network, is the basic 'organization of the living'. This first point is fundamental when looking to transform organizations to unleash leaders. It is a clue to a new structure and behaviour for organizations.

The second conclusion Maturana came to was that the nervous system is not only self-organizing but also continually self-referring, so that perception cannot be viewed as the representation of an external reality but must be understood as the continual creation of new relationships within the network. Again this is a concept that is fundamental to our organizations.

From this premise Maturana then postulated that the process of circular organization itself, even without a nervous system, is identical to the process of cognition. 'Living systems are cognitive systems.'[13] In other words they are knowing or acquiring knowledge. This is the basis of true learning organizations. Peter Senge's idea of the learning organization has been difficult to put into practice. This work can, I believe, enable Senge's vision to become real everywhere.

From the 1970s on, Maturana worked with Francisco Varela and they focused on organization rather than structure. They concluded that 'in a living system *the product of its operation is its own organization*'.[14] This statement is the third fundamental point from Maturana that will enable us to build new memes for the development of organizations. For instead of just building hierarchies because that's what we've done in the past, we can focus on the operation, the objectives and the purpose of the organization. This goes beyond business process re-engineering because it will result in transforming the structures. To those who I hear shouting, 'We've done that', the reply has to be, 'No, you haven't', because you still have a picture of what an organization should look like from the old meme. This new organization will require radical thinking similar to that of the following example.

James Lovelock formulated a model of self-organization in his idea that the Earth was a whole, living self-organizing system. The process of self-regulation is key to his ideas and he knew he was breaking away from the conventional world view. He said: 'Consider Gaia theory as an alternative to the conventional wisdom that sees the Earth as a dead planet made of inanimate rocks, ocean and atmosphere, and merely inhabited by life. Consider it as a real system, comprising all of life, and all of its environment tightly coupled so as to form a self-regulatory entity.'[15]

If we saw our working organizations as self-regulatory, there would not be a need for all the managers to control them. Riccardo Semler showed this in his book *Maverick*, which told how he ran his business without control.

According to Maturana, the behaviour of a living organism is determined. However, rather than being determined by outside forces, it is determined by the organism's own structure – a structure formed by a succession of autonomous structural changes. Thus the behaviour is both determined and free. Yet this does not mean it is predictable.

During the 1980s Warwick University found that change in organizations came from outside forces. Yet organizations' responses have been limited by their structures. But new ideas of the kind I have been outlining from ecology have made it possible to realize that the behaviour that takes place inside an organization is actually determined by its structure. In addition, if the structure is inflexible, the organization will have huge difficulty to cope in a fast-changing environment. According to the theory of evolution, the organization will evolve, and survival of the fittest will ensure those that remain are the best. Is this occurring or are we seeing the best people leaving because of frustration and a rigid boss? Part of the classical theory of evolution is the idea that, in the course of change and under the pressure of natural selection, organisms will gradually adapt to their environment until they reach a fit that is good enough for survival. In the new systems view, by contrast, evolutionary change is seen as the result of life's inherent tendency to create novelty, which may or may not be accompanied by adaptation to changing environmental conditions.

The Gaia theory – developed by Lovelock and based on seeing the Earth as a self-organizing system – leads us to question the narrow Darwinian concept of adaptation. It would seem that evolution cannot be limited to the adaptation of organisms to their environment, because the environment itself is a network of living systems capable of adaptation and creativity. This leads Capra to ask: 'So which adapts to which?' He answers: 'Each to the other – they co-evolve.'[16]

James Lovelock says: 'So closely coupled is the evolution of living organisms with the evolution of the environment that together they constitute a single evolutionary process.'[17] In other words, we look at the whole picture.

In organizations also, this concept is paramount, in fact it is the missing factor in organizational development. We send individuals on training programmes to learn and change but they return to their organization that has not done either. Downsizing and playing with the structure is insufficient. Individuals and organizations need to co-evolve. In many cases neither are doing more than 'pretending' to change.

Another concept from ecology that needs to be applied to our organizations is 'symbiosis'. After a century of wars it is clear that all larger organisms, including ourselves, are learning that destructive practices do not work in the long run. In the end the aggressors always destroy themselves, making way for others who know how to cooperate and get along. Life is actually much less a competitive struggle for survival than a triumph of cooperation and creativity. For human beings, the role of language in human evolution was not so much to exchange ideas, as to increase the ability to cooperate. Cooperation and partnerships will become increasingly important in a global world made up of interconnected networks. Fundamental to cooperation and partnership is trust – something that is often missing from organizations but that needs to be built up to enable interconnections.

In ecological terms a living system is a multiple, interconnected network whose components are constantly changing, being transformed and replaced by other components. There is great fluidity and flexibility in the network, which allows the system to respond by rearranging its patterns of connectivity. Yet we continue to try and operate from inflexible structures in working organizations with inflexible processes. In ecology, structural changes are acts of cognition, which means development is always associated with learning. In our organizations learning and development needs to happen for both human beings and the organization.

Looking at living systems provides us with a conceptual framework for the link between ecological communities and human communities, such as organizations. Both are living systems – networks open to the flow of energy and resources – their structures are determined by their histories; they are intelligent because of the cognitive component within the process of life. Yet we try to build and run our organizations as machines tied to an old paradigm.

Of course there are also differences between the two in that humans have language, culture and consciousness, and are self-aware. Ecosystems do not have justice and democracy, but neither do they have greed and dishonesty. We cannot learn about these from ecosystems, but what we can learn is how to use the principles as guidelines to build sustainable human organizations as communities. We are all part of the new world view. This is where the new memes will grow.

A sustainable human community is aware of the multiple relationships among its members. Nourishing the community means nourishing those relationships. Lack of flexibility manifests itself as stress. In particular stress will occur when one or more variables of the system are pushed to their extreme values, which induces increased rigidity throughout the system. Temporary stress is a normal aspect of life, but prolonged stress is harmful and destructive to the system and is all too common in organizations today.

The final lesson from ecology is that of diversity in organizations. Diversity should be regarded as positive. Too many organizations say they support diversity but in reality they want compliance. Diversity here means many different relationships, many different approaches to the same problem. A diverse community is a resilient community, capable of adapting to changing situations.

These are some of the basic principles of ecology – interdependence, partnership, flexibility and diversity and, as a consequence of all these, sustainability. Organizations in the twenty-first century will have to understand these principles and develop themselves accordingly. It will involve more than saying the words because they are fashionable and will require living the new ideas and thinking. For a start, our world view will have to change to take on board these new memes, but the question is 'when', not 'if'. For these memes are already appearing in different places and in individuals who want a different way to live and work.

These are some of the ideas behind the new thinking emerging in the world. What is the significance of these developments for the future of organizations? When we look at these new ideas together they afford a wide transformation of our understanding of the individual and the world that he or she perceives. These developments together form the beginning of a critical mass that will result in drastic change for both individuals and organizations.

We should still acknowledge the period of scientific endeavour of Descartes, Newton and Galileo with its rationality, desire for control and manipulation over nature and its mechanistic world view, for it led to advances in technological hardware and the rise of the professional manager from the Industrial Revolution. But today we are evolving toward greater fulfilment of human potential and purpose to improve organizations and societies so that people are fulfilled in spiritual as well as material ways. The Industrial Age and with it management in hierarchies is coming to an end.

The resistance will be huge. Philosopher David Bohm describes the challenge: 'The forms that we have in our world view are charged with tremendous energy, and presumably when that world view is challenged . . . a tremendous explosion may take place and people fight over it to the death . . . Nevertheless it may be necessary to challenge these world views if they are wrong. There is a risk in doing so, but there is also perhaps a greater risk in not doing so, because if we go on with a fixed, rigid world view it will lead us to the edge of the abyss, right?'[18] We saw examples of the dangers in the older civilizations. This time, if we have a framework for the new memes the outcome can be different.

There is still a long way to go as we begin to move into a new paradigm with old-paradigm thinking. For some, the future is the Information Age. This is a false assumption as the influx of information is part of the shifting process – not the end state. At present, we still treat information as hardware technologies, mass production, narrow economic models of efficiency and competition, all of which are remnants of the Industrial Age. We have yet to take account of the new stage of human development. We also have to make sure that when we look at transforming organizations, we don't make the same mistake. For the new paradigm includes human development and this is the last piece of the puzzle to enable us to see the new paradigm that needs to be taken on board in organizations.

The psychology/social science contribution

A group of social scientists came together in 1946 to form the Tavistock Institute of Human Relations in London. The pioneers recognized the need for a new model of organization that would replace the traditional rational, bureaucratic hierarchy. During the 1970s they already recognized the impact technology would make. One of the key individuals at the Tavistock Clinic was Eric Trist who told a conference in 1971:

> The problem was not of simply 'adjusting' people to technology nor technology to people but of organizing the interface so that the best match could be obtained between them . . . This encompassed the enterprise as a whole – in relation to its environment – as well as its primary work groups and intervening sub-systems. It was necessary to change the basic model in which organizational theory had been conceived.[19]

The Tavistock team were greatly influenced by Austrian biologist von Bertalanffy and by the ideas from cybernetics as mentioned already. Trist added to his conference speech: 'The more complex, fast-changing, interdependent world growing up in the wake of the second industrial revolution is rapidly rendering obsolete and maladaptive many of the values, organizational structures and work practices brought about by the first. In fact something like their opposite seems to be required.'[20]

What the Tavistock team were proposing was to increase the ability of the individuals to participate in decision-making and in influencing the work environment. In other words, they wanted to see the development of leadership throughout organizations.

In the field of psychology individuals were breaking away from Fraudism and developing a more positive contribution to human development. Carl Jung believed that through the humanity in all of us we are connected and can transcend the differences of race, culture and beliefs. His main theory held that the personality we acquire through our upbringing and social conditioning is only part of what makes us who we are.

For Jung, within each individual was a deeper, wiser being that was unique and the centre of consciousness. This he called the 'eternal Self', expressed when all parts of our complex personality are integrated. When this occurs, Jung believes, we can relate to others in a more authentic and meaningful way. For me, leadership is a large part of this. So how do we become 'Self'? Jung recognized the process as difficult but possible through a 'map' with signposts in our deep unconsciousness that will take us on an inner journey of evolution. This is why leadership has to involve this inner journey and is different for every human being.

On the other side of the world, human development for Abraham Maslow was based on the attainment of what he called 'self-actualization.' Throughout his life, Maslow argued for a philosophy of humanity that recognized and developed the human capacity for creativity, compassion, ethics, love, spirituality and other human traits. He put this forward as a scientist following testing, hypothesizing and debating. So why has self-actualization been so difficult to attain?

Maslow says: 'We fear out highest possibilities (as well as our lowest ones). We are generally afraid to become that which we can glimpse in our most perfect moments. We enjoy and thrill to the god-like possibilities we see in ourselves. And yet we simultaneously shiver with weakness, awe and fear before these very same possibilities.'[21] To develop leadership we have to begin with an inward journey to deal with self-limiting beliefs and fears. The tendency is to distract ourselves from doing this by chasing external goals. Why is this?

In the book *In Search of Leaders* I showed that throughout history there have been a succession of world views or paradigms based on our perception of reality. Each of these has expressed the thinking and spirit of its time, and each having a profound effect on the individual and society as a whole.

Today the main world view in the west is one where the Earth is one body made of rock and dust in an immense universe of material bodies with no meaning. The implication of this view is that we human beings are insignificant. The universe is totally indifferent to the individual's hopes, aspirations, moral views and fate. Those individuals who strive for power, control and material wealth are accountable to no one.

This world view reached its complete development during the nineteenth century. It has affected the lives of most of us and keeps us feeling isolated. Our hardest task is to trust – other individuals and the Universe. The feeling of isolation is immense, and some individuals may feel suicidal. Embedded in this world view are thoughts and beliefs from past world views and in particular from religion.

Western religion encouraged the 'work ethic' and the fear of being too happy. We fear as well as desire self-actualization because we've been taught that there must be some suffering, guilt and unhappiness. Therefore pleasure and self-fulfilment are often tainted with feelings of 'any moment the bubble will burst' or 'I don't deserve this'.

Together, the feeling of isolation and the fear of happiness keep us from our true potential. In transforming organizations this issue must be included because organizations are made up of people. When they can express themselves fully and authentically, leadership comes forth. A new movement of self-expression is emerging yet before us.

When Maslow wrote on leadership he described it as the action of someone who is doing something they love and cannot separate themselves from their task or duty. 'The concept of the task or the vocation or the duty becoming part of the self, defining a necessary part, a sine qua non part, this I think is difficult to understand in the culture which cuts these things apart and makes dichotomies out of them.'[22]

The present situation

When we look at these influences from science, ecology and social science during the last 50 to 100 years, we can see the edges and even the centre of the new paradigm that will enable us to resolve the issue of truly transforming organizations. Each of the subjects of learning we have covered contribute to a new way forward. Together they form a new memecomplex. The picture that evolves now is one where the following elements will be fundamental.

From quantum

Interrelationships, interconnections and a network of relationships are crucial to our understanding of the world today.

From systems

Look at the whole not the parts; see the world as interconnected; distinguish pattern from physical structure; and recognize a need to include human well-being in the future. Interacting fields of energy in open systems involving communicating without being tied to rigid processes are the most effective.

From chaos

There is disorder and irregularity everywhere when you look for it; systems are sensitive to even minute change, which can have huge effects. There is a need to shake off the second law of thermodynamics – organizations do not have to decline. We can never know or understand everything but we can find wonder and awe from all around.

From ecology

We need to add community and network. The circular organization is the basis for all living systems; a network pattern is needed to help, produce and transform the whole; within the system is 'knowing' and the need for acquiring knowledge and self-regulation. The structure leads to the behaviour of the organization. Diversity, creativity, learning, flexibility and cooperation are developed so that the system co-evolves with its environment. Individuals are not separate from the rest of nature or each other. Individuals and organizations need to co-evolve together.

From social science

There is a need to change the basic model in which organizational theory has been conceived. Structures, values and work practices will be turned on their heads. 'Self actualization' or the 'eternal Self' is the goal for human beings that should be as important as financial goals. Having purpose and meaning for work is fundamental, while creativity and leadership should be expressed throughout. The individual should feel part of a larger, conscious, spiritual whole. Individuals should trust their intuition and instinct. We should be humble but not limit our potential.

This is the universal framework from which to transform organizations. The new memecomplex will look like this (Figure 6.1). We now have to put this framework into a model to transform organizations that will unleash leadership. This is the next challenge.

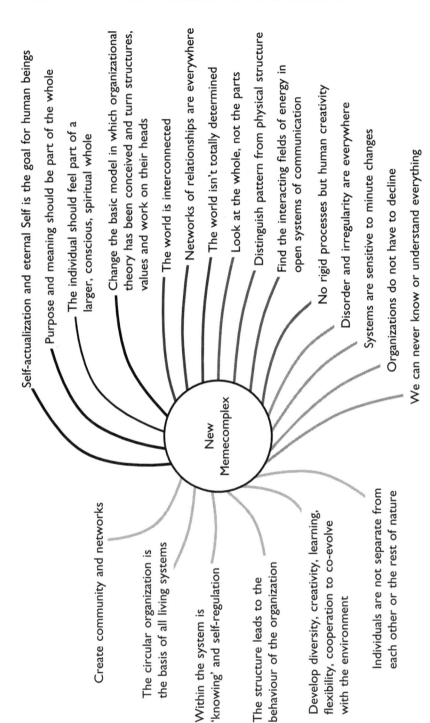

Self-actualization and eternal Self is the goal for human beings

Purpose and meaning should be part of the whole

The individual should feel part of a larger, conscious, spiritual whole

Change the basic model in which organizational theory has been conceived and turn structures, values and work on their heads

The world is interconnected

Networks of relationships are everywhere

The world isn't totally determined

Look at the whole, not the parts

Distinguish pattern from physical structure

Find the interacting fields of energy in open systems of communication

No rigid processes but human creativity

Disorder and irregularity are everywhere

Systems are sensitive to minute changes

Organizations do not have to decline

We can never know or understand everything

New Memecomplex

Create community and networks

The circular organization is the basis of all living systems

Within the system is 'knowing' and self-regulation

The structure leads to the behaviour of the organization

Develop diversity, creativity, learning, flexibility, cooperation to co-evolve with the environment

Individuals are not separate from each other or the rest of nature

Figure 6.1   The New Memecomplex for the Twenty-first Century

7

Building a New Model for Organizations

You never change things by fighting the existing reality. To change something, build a new model that makes the existing model obsolete.

Buckminster Fuller

*T*he first stage of unleashing leaders is complete. We have a framework – a synthesis depicting the world of which organizations are a part. Throughout this chapter we will keep this framework or memecomplex in our mind as we try to build a new model for organizations to enable everyone to practise their leadership. Where do we begin?

Looking into the future, two academics from Henley Management Centre said: 'Tomorrow's dominant form of business organization will differ from that of today at its very foundation – in its structure.'[1] However, the question many ask is, 'Change to what?' Before we try to answer that, we need to look at the whole concept of structure.

Structure

The word 'structure' means complex construction. Over the years, when I've asked directors to draw their organizations they come up with an array of structures, each director saying that their diagram is correct even though they work for the same organization. When asking the same from managers the tendency is to draw two diagrams – the one they are told by their directors and the one they see as the reality from their everyday experience. In other words, structure in organizations is complex and fraught with contradiction. Does this matter?

It does when we learn from the new memecomplex that the behaviour of an organization is determined by its structure. This is formed by a sequence of structural changes that determines the whole system's behaviour. Ecologist Maturana called this behaviour 'structure-deterimined'. Rather than behaviour being determined by outside forces, Maturana believes it is determined by the organism's own structure. Now we can see that there is a distinction between reacting to something outside and change that is determined by the structure.

An example of this is the rise in mergers and acquisitions through globalization. An organization we shall call x reacts to global competition by entering into a merger, for example with z. The reality is that rather than a merger you end up with two organizations fighting each other because they have two different structures and ways of behaving. What happens next is a battle of dominance with sometimes one, in this case x, coming out on top. This dominant partner x then tries to make the other, z, like itself – even when it was attracted to z because of its differences – and conflict arises with resentment.

In many cases neither organization changes because of the different structures holding them back and behaviour of the people. This can be seen in recent mergers between German and US companies. Some will argue that it is differences in culture both in nationality and in the two companies that are to blame. Culture is important but the cultures came following the structure. Therefore are we saying that if we change the structure, culture will change? This is difficult because most organizations have only tinkered with their structure and not really transformed them. For example, the presence of over 100 women MPs in the House of Commons since 1997 has had little impact in changing its structure. However, when we look at organizations that have a network structure the behaviour within them is different and leadership can be seen and felt throughout. In the rest we still have flatter hierarchies and hierarchical thinking with the outcome of limited change in behaviour. Is there an alternative to the hierarchy? We know from the memecomplex framework that the future is about interconnections, interrelationships, community, self-regulation, learning, diversity, cooperation and networks of relationships that can deal with chaos and fast change. The preferred structure for these new memes is a network or web organization with a circular structure rather than pyramid.

The network structure

Gareth Morgan put forward a network organization in his book *Creative Organization Theory* (see Figure 7.1).[2] What is interesting is that he compares this network with matrix and project-team types of organization, thus showing that the latter two are not sufficiently different to the hierarchy structure. This has implications for many organizations that regard themselves to have changed and model themselves on a matrix or project-team structure.

In a matrix structure, the project manager maintains a team against a background of functional activities. The structure encourages learning and a strong technical base but can evoke a conflict of priorities for functional managers. This often happens because there is still a hierarchy above them, making demands in functional formats. Above this, the top of the hierarchy is still strong in influencing the rest of the organization and with it the 'thinking'. In a matrix structure, the emphasis is on performance and results. The behaviour and culture results in high task-orientation, which leads to individuals being measured only by target achievement.

In the network structure being proposed here, the top team are in the centre reaching out and are more visible and accountable. In Morgan's network structure, customers are viewed as part of the network, and the organization and its customers are seen as one whole system. The network will be constantly changing as it adjusts to the changing needs of

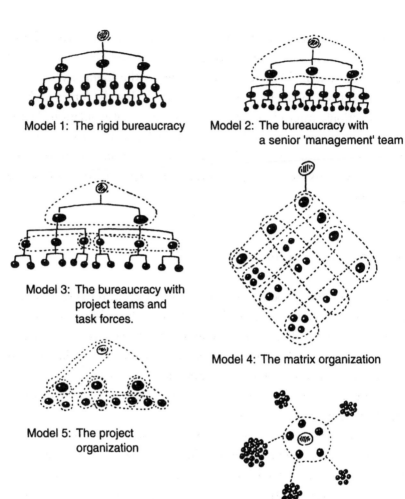

Model 1: The rigid bureaucracy

Model 2: The bureaucracy with
a senior 'management' team

Model 3: The bureaucracy with
project teams and
task forces.

Model 4: The matrix organization

Model 5: The project
organization

Model 6: The loosely-coupled
organic network

Figure 7.1   The Emergence of the Networked Organization as developed by Gareth Morgan[2]
© Sage Publications, 1989

the hub while it services its customer base. Flows of information around the network will be vital as it deals with ongoing changes.

In the circular structure, interconnections and networking communication will be dependent on the people, not the technology. Fundamental is the realization that the more turbulent and unpredictable the

Figure 7.2   The Emergence of the Network Organization

environment, the more the organization needs to be structured in a way to enable it to respond dynamically.

Sproull and Keisler, in their book *Connections – New Ways of Working in the Networked Organization*, set out four principles needed for the network organization to work.[3] The first is that everyone should communicate via the network. Although the use of email will be important, face-to-face communication in and across teams will also be vital. What should disappear are the back-to-back meetings managers seem to have more and more of, with few outcomes. Second, there should be open access to people and information. This should be based on the assumption that every employee has something relevant to contribute. The third principle is that forums should be provided through which people can work together. Forums are not meetings and should not be set and run as such. Finally, policies and incentives to encourage information exchange should be in place and practice.

Let's stop here and focus on your organization for a few minutes.

• Take a piece of paper and draw your organization as you see it today.
• Identify and list the patterns of behaviour in it.
• Now on another piece of paper draw your organization as a circular network described as above. Be as creative and visionary as you want.

- Identify and list the behaviour in it as you think it would be, around it and connected to it. What are the main differences in the two?

Implications

There are fundamental changes stemming from a network structure. The first is a shift in power. In the hierarchy, power is based on position. In a network structure, power is based on what and who people know. Communication in a network allows people to bypass traditional information gatekeepers and access information sources directly. With open communication, power is distributed to all.

The second implication is that career ladders will disappear in a network. Instead people will be able to move around with ease to different parts without attaching to it failure or promotion. This enables organizations to get people 'out of boxes' to work in different parts of the structure, including working with customers and suppliers or on projects. All this will enhance personal development away from the normal training programmes. To encourage personal growth for everyone, all employees including directors could develop coaching and facilitating skills to help and support each other. In the past this development has tended to be for managers or 'specialists' only. Already, we can see how this real change in structure can bring about real change in behaviour.

The third implication will make it possible for service to the customer to become a reality. Network structures are about inclusion and when suppliers, customers and others on the periphery become part of a holistic network, they become part of the organization and its environment. This is very different from a hierarchical structure.

A similar structure is that of a web. Sally Helgesen introduced this structure in her book *Web of Inclusion*. 'In architectural terms, the most obvious characteristics of the web are that it builds from the centre out and that this building is a never-ending process – spinning new tendrils of connection and strengthening existing ones,' She adds: 'The structures were discernible mainly in the daily rhythms of how the businesses were run – how time was used, what titles people assumed, how physical space was allotted, the means by which people talked to one another and reached decisions.'[1]

Most of these web structures were set up by women so Helgesen explored why this was. She concluded: 'It was fairly clear to see why the women in the studies had structured their companies in innovative ways, for they came as outsiders to positions of leadership in the public sphere.'[5] In other words, the memes for seeing an organization only as a hierarchy were not as strong for them. This point is important and worth linking to discoveries made in the earlier chapter on ancient civilizations. The greatest influence on the western world in particular were the Greeks whose memes are still around today. In Greek society Aristotle divided the world into a hierarchy with men at the top and women below. For thousands of years this was believed and women were considered inferior and left out of political and business organizations. In the 1970s, in particular, the position of women in society was challenged by feminists who believed equality meant accepting women at the top of these hierarchical organizations. During the 1980s many of us fought our way up them, often losing part of our own identity and feeling alien. I now believe that the reason for this was that we do not carry the memes that are so entrenched in men who have built and run these organizations for so long. Instead women today will find it easier to create new structures.

Helgesen also adds: 'The web is particularly suited as an architecture for our era because its very design mirrors the structure of our primary technology, the integrated network.'[6] The web structure is one I personally am comfortable with and have used to structure my own organization. It has enabled us to focus on making continual connections, and also enables our customers to connect with one another. It is as Erich Jantsch wrote: 'In life, the issue is not control but dynamic connectiveness.'[7]

Whether a web or a network, the new organizations I am describing are circular rather than pyramid in form, enabling communication, involvement and power to be present throughout. They also unleash leadership everywhere. It means that whatever your role in the organization, leadership becomes your personal challenge. When we break free from the hierarchy, the words of Tom Peters can no longer be ignored: 'The chief reason for our failure in world class competition is our failure to tap our work force's potential.'[8] This potential will be realized only when individuals break free from the hierarchy in their thinking and behaviour – as well as its physical boundaries. Then leadership will be unleashed and expressed by all.

There now exists an alternative to the hierarchy that is aligned with our framework:

- The circular organization is the basis of all living systems, enabling human beings to connect with nature again; after being separate since the times of the Greeks, which was reinforced through the mechanistic world view of Newton;
- The circular organization creates community and networks, enabling work to have purpose, meaning and direction where the individual feels part of a larger consciousness;
- The circular organization enables leadership to emerge and other changes in behaviour such as flexibility, creativity, cooperation, self-actualization and learning without rigid processes or decline;
- The circular organization can respond to constant dynamic change and irregularity through co-evolving with its environment and self-regulation;
- The circular organization will flow with energy and communication;
- The board of directors in the circular organization will focus on the whole, not on broken-up parts, and accept they will never know everything.
- Everyone in the circular organization will see pattern rather than physical structure, and leadership will be unleashed throughout where the focus will be on learning.

The future will be circular organizations and they are already emerging. As for those who have been a hierarchy organization for many years, the challenge will be about whether those at the top and in the middle of the hierarchy really want to change it.

Learning

The new structures are very different from the hierarchy and have distinct advantages, one of the most important being that they allow learning. In fact this ability for learning is so important we will focus on it now.

The network enables Peter Senge's 'learning organization' to become a reality and leadership to be expressed throughout. Organizational learning occurs when experiences are shared from each and every interaction among employees, with customers or clients, with suppliers and even with competitors. Organizational learning is often blocked in hierarchies and occurs only in a part of the structure. This blockage affects the organization's success in the future. 'A learning organization is continually expanding its capacity to create its future' (Senge, 1990).[9]

It is obvious that in a fast-changing world the learning must be greater, not just so that the organization can respond and survive but also to have this capacity to develop and create the future. In a hierarchy where information gets stuck, learning is very limited. In the new structure information flows, and learning not only occurs at individual level but also at team level. In fact very often the learning is greater in teams.

Learning includes the transfer of knowledge between individuals and shared mental models. Mental models affect what we 'see' in that two people with different models can look at the same thing or situation and see two different items or problems. These mental models then determine how we take action. The problem is that they lie below our level of awareness. The outcome is that individuals say they believe in empowerment but their actions are not consistent with this because it isn't what they really believe. Addressing these deep models is crucial to learning.

Learning also allows flexibility in the network to respond to disturbances or stimuli from the environment. This leads to the patterns of connections changing and rearranging themselves, thus resulting in teams moving around and forming new teams. The structural changes described here are acts of cognition and this means that organizational development is always linked to learning. Therefore developing leadership in individuals should go hand in hand with developing the organization. This I believe is why so much 'training' in leadership has been limited.

Senge said that in a learning organization, leaders are designers, stewards and teachers. He added that they were responsible for building organizations where people continually expand their capacities to understand complexity, clarity, vision and improve mental models. In other words, they were responsible for learning. In this context learning is perceived as an 'active' process. I would like to add something else to the understanding of learning.

Inner knowledge

Inside all human beings as well as knowledge that can be used or shared there is something else that is equally important. It is an inner wisdom that appears to have more to do with the spirit than the brain. This wisdom is an intuitive 'knowing' that often cannot be explained with logic or in rational terms. In the new structure the sharing of this wisdom can be included as part of the expression of leadership. The problem is that most individuals are not used to owning their inner wisdom and when they do the experience feels very different to using brain knowledge.

When inner wisdom is expressed it seems to come from a quiet place with the feeling of calm and 'just knowing' filling the body. The ability to tap into this inner wisdom seems to be stronger in some than others. However, this ability should not be feared and trusted by those using it. What we do know for sure is that learning is more complex than we understand at present, and it is fundamental to leadership. Senge saw learning as the role of managers but here it is the role of every employee as they each are leaders in the new structure.

The process of learning

Learning is more complex than we often assume, and as a component of leadership needs further understanding. Jean Piaget found two distinct processes of learning in his studies.[10] The first involves taking in information through the process of 'assimilation'. This is done through lectures, books and conventional school and business school learning. The second process of learning involves the individual experiencing internal change in their beliefs, attitudes and ideas. This process he calls 'learning by accommodation' and requires much more than conventional teaching and training. It is an experiential process where individuals participate not only with their intellect but also with their heart while accepting that the final outcome will not be known. All they will know is that they will be different when the journey ends. Learning by accommodation is fundamental to unleashing leaders.

Learning by accommodation will also be required to deal with the change in thinking and beliefs that has evaded us so far. In organizations where individuals believe they have changed, ask people these questions:

- Do you really believe that people are totally trustworthy?
- Do you really believe that people seek responsibility and accountability?
- Do you really believe that people seek meaning and purpose in their work?
- Do you really believe that people want to learn and develop?
- Do you really believe that all people have leadership potential?

These beliefs are fundamental if we want organizations to unleash leaders. Chris Argyris has explored beliefs in depth and found a huge gap between the beliefs people professed and the beliefs they actually expressed especially when under pressure or threat.[11] He found a deeply ingrained master programme of behaviour that he claims is similar across cultures and classes. This behaviour includes a defensive reflex action, blaming others when things go wrong, saving face and striving to maintain control. People are so good at this that many don't realize they are doing it.

We now know these beliefs are in part a result of our memes, including those fighting to maintain the hierarchy, present power base and control. The fundamental point of Argyris' argument is that this negative behaviour prevents learning. If we are going to unleash leaders everywhere in organizations then we have to use a process that addresses all these beliefs.

Argyris also found a distinction in processing information that affects learning. He describes what he calls 'single loop learning' as a solution for single loop problems. Single loop learning is information based, so cutting a cost is based on the information that costs need to be reduced and the simplest way is to cut them. An example is when someone cuts costs to meet a budget. Whereas double loop learning goes beyond absorbing information. It involves beliefs and perceptions and occurs when underlying assumptions are questioned to elicit information that enables root causes to be tackled and permanent change to result. There are two points worth noting from Argyris' ideas. The first is that we tend to see more single loop learning in the hierarchy among managers. Second, only by challenging assumptions and beliefs will real transformation occur. If unleashing leaders is the goal, a process towards it needs to include tackling these assumptions and beliefs that goes deeper than conventional training.

Organizations and individuals who use a defensive process deny responsibility for circumstances and resist learning. This is why Argyris says changing an organization's systems or structure to date has been an essentially single loop activity where little if anything really changes. The lack of change will often be denied by those at the top of the organization and leads Argyris to conclude that being blind to reality is part of the problem of executives and managers. He describes this blindness as comparable to a fast train coming toward you in a tunnel but, like rabbits in the glare of the headlights, realizing the danger takes the impact for any reaction. Argyris found that when individuals become aware of the beliefs and perceptions blinding executives to the reality then people can begin to change. The work by Argyris shows how difficult learning and development is and how people development has to go hand in hand with organizational development if we are to unleash leaders.

The measure of organizations

There is another barrier to learning, identified by Arie de Geus as how organizations are judged. Outsiders – for example, as the City – judge and measure in economic terms such as return on investment and capital assets; whereas inside the organization success depends on how we interconnect and work with other human beings developing knowledge. De Geus says: 'I'm inclined to believe that the sharp difference between these two definitions – the economic definition and the learning company definition – lies at the core of the crisis which managers face today.'[12]

In the new structure it will be easier to assess connections and learning. Within structure there is 'pattern' that includes the regular way things are done. In the circular network or web structure the pattern of behaviour includes leadership and learning. This behaviour will be visible not only in economic performance but also in teams, relationships with customers and so on, and can be included in company reports. In the hierarchy, leadership and learning are both limited and so cannot be so readily included. It's learning and leadership *acquired* that need to be added to the bottom line. This can be shown in terms of value rather than measured (we need to break away from the belief that if something can't be measured it isn't of value).

Arie de Geus goes on to say that those who focus only on economic definitions are the 'experts' and academics who suggest the heart of the company is solely its economic activity that it pursues to stay alive; while individuals see the core of the company is its existence as a work community where success and profits are the result of individuals working together with purpose and personal gratification from their work. In the network organization the aim is to build a community.

Hierarchy versus community

Hierarchies create a culture of competitiveness to enable people to fight to the top whereby a few gain the greatest benefits. To maintain hierarchies, the environment in which they exist must be stable.

In a community, on the other hand, people work together, are supportive rather than competitive, take responsibility and share values, and the benefits are for all. Here, change and transformation in the environment is okay because everyone can respond together. The interconnections between individuals and customers or suppliers and the environment is much stronger, enabling much greater customer satisfaction. Knowledge and information can flow freely without management slowing down the process.

Knowledge in the network

Knowledge has become the most important factor in economic life. It is the chief ingredient of what we buy and sell, the raw material with which we work. Intellectual capital – not natural resources, machinery or even financial capital – has become the one indispensable asset of organizations.

Thomas Stewart, 1997[13]

What is intellectual capital? It's knowledge and information – but it's also much more. It's the ideas, creativity, innovation, imagination and know-how of people. It's the collective brain power of the workforce and outside parties. If given the chance, it is what makes a team or organization great.

Helgesen links knowledge to the new circular structure when she writes:

In the knowledge-based economy that Peter Drucker foresees as our future, the real value of an organization will lie in its people's ability to think, to process information, to evolve creative solutions to complex problems. And people cannot simply *think* creatively and well if they do not feel valued, if they do not feel a sense of ownership of their work, if they do not have the freedom to give full scope to their talents.[14]

Later she strongly says:

> . . . It also demands that organizations move beyond the old Industrial Era mentality that perceives a dichotomy between what is efficient and what is humane . . . The architecture of the web of inclusion offers us such a source . . . The old organizational architecture, with its implicit assumptions of an underlying hierarchical order, its emphasis on rank, boundary and division, has outlived its usefulness.[15]

Knowledge cannot flow and interconnect in the old structure.

Knowledge includes knowing

In the network organization the notion of epistemology – understanding the process of knowing – has to be included. This knowing isn't just the left brain full of facts and logic; but includes the right brain with its capacity for emotional intelligence, intuition and awareness of the world. Even more so, 'knowing' can be described as the wisdom of the soul for it comes from inside us rather than from an intellectual source. It is that moment when we say: 'I can't prove it, I just know.' In the future this knowing will become more important in a chaotic world and we need to learn to trust it.

In the past, it was the bosses in the hierarchy who said they knew more and had the answers. Today the opposite is true. Peter Senge said: 'In an increasingly, dynamic, interdependent and unpredictable world, it is simply no longer possible for anyone to "figure it all out at the top". The old model, "the top thinks and the locals act", must now give way to integrating thinking and acting at all levels.'[16] We all know this, but it really isn't happening in most places of work.

Fundamental to what Senge is saying here is the issue of trust – which stems from beliefs. Do those at the top of organizations *really* believe that they don't have all the answers? Will those at the top trust the knowledge of others no matter where they are in the organization?

Are those at the top willing to share power, leadership, knowledge and work as a team themselves? Are they committed to the new structure? Leadership expressed throughout in hierarchies is extremely difficult if at all possible, but in the circular network made up of teams or clusters, the impossible becomes possible. Behaviour is dependent on structure. Are those at the top and individuals who were managers committed to the new structure? If not, then we know why. They want to maintain their control over others and to serve themselves.

Change in behaviour

In the past the goal was to move up the hierarchy and have more people reporting to you. People were motivated by material rewards and fear of punishment. Work goals were determined by your manager in the hierarchy and decisions were made at the top. The focus was internal and based on maintaining order.

In the network organization there is a true learning environment. Income is tied to capability and accomplishments rather than position. Leadership rather than management is required and able to be expressed throughout.

Teams and clusters become the building blocks and these move around and change without the need for managers. Teams are excellent for learning and creativity. Instead of just focusing on how to resolve problems, teams can focus on what needs to happen and how to achieve it. Individuals are no longer employees of the organization – they *are* the organization and they make a difference.

This new structure is:

a multiply-interconnected network whose components are con-stantly changing, being transformed and replaced by other components. There is great fluidity and flexibility in this network, which allows the system to respond to disturbances or stimuli from the environment in a special way. Certain disturbances trigger specific structural change, i.e. changes in the connectivity throughout the network. This is a distributive phenomenon. The entire network responds to a selected disturbance by reorganising its patterns of connectivity.[17]

Capra

What Capra is showing us here is how a network organization is fluid, moving, responding and dynamic. For me this shows energy and life. It is the difference of going into one of those rare organizations and feeling its 'buzz' or energy whereas many organizations will have none.

The ecological link

What are being described above by Capra are living systems. Whenever we encounter living systems we see networks. The understanding of living systems provides us with the means of understanding the link between ecological communities and human communities. Both are living systems that exhibit the same basic principles of organization. The problem we've had to overcome is the separation of ourselves from the rest of life that began with Aristotle's classification of life and was enforced by the ideas of Descartes and Newton who saw mankind as separate and the masters of nature.

With our present understanding of life as expressed in the new memecomplex all organizations become networks of interconnections open to the flows of energy and resources; their structures are determined by their histories of structural changes; and they are intelligent because of the cognitive dimension inherent in the process of life.

One of the crucial differences in human from other ecological organizations is our capacity for language. The fundamental role of language is to enable us to cooperate, leading to the generation of ideas, learning and sustainability. A sustainable human community is aware of the multiple relationships among its members. It allows diversity rather than compliance that means many different relationships and many different approaches to the same problem. A diverse community is a resilient community, capable of adapting to changing situations. This is very different from most of our present organizations where lack of flexibility has manifested itself as stress – the illness of the 1980s and 1990s.

Synergy

The aim of the network organization where teams form the basis is to produce synergy; that is, the results of the work of these teams is greater than if they were individuals working alone. In *Creating Top Flight Teams* I developed a model (Figure 7.3) for teams, which was called the 'synergy chain', in which developing the interconnected links produced synergy.[18]

For Abraham Maslow, synergy was a culture in organizations where what was beneficial for the individual was beneficial for everyone. In teams this culture is developed through the synergy chain model and has been effective in several countries where I have worked and across teams made up of different nationalities.

Synergy became increasingly important in Maslow's work on organizational theory as he saw more and more cultures where success could only occur at the expense of others. The behaviour is a result of the hierarchy structure. In the new network organization the focus is on pattern rather than physical structure. The pattern is how individuals organise themselves to achieve something that matters and this is done through teams working alone or with other teams.

Resistance

Finally we need to address the issue of resistance to this transformation of organizations. Marilyn Ferguson wrote: 'New paradigms are nearly always received with coolness, every mockery or hostility. Those with vested interests fight the change. The shift demands such a different view of things that established leaders are often the last to be won over, if at all.'[19]

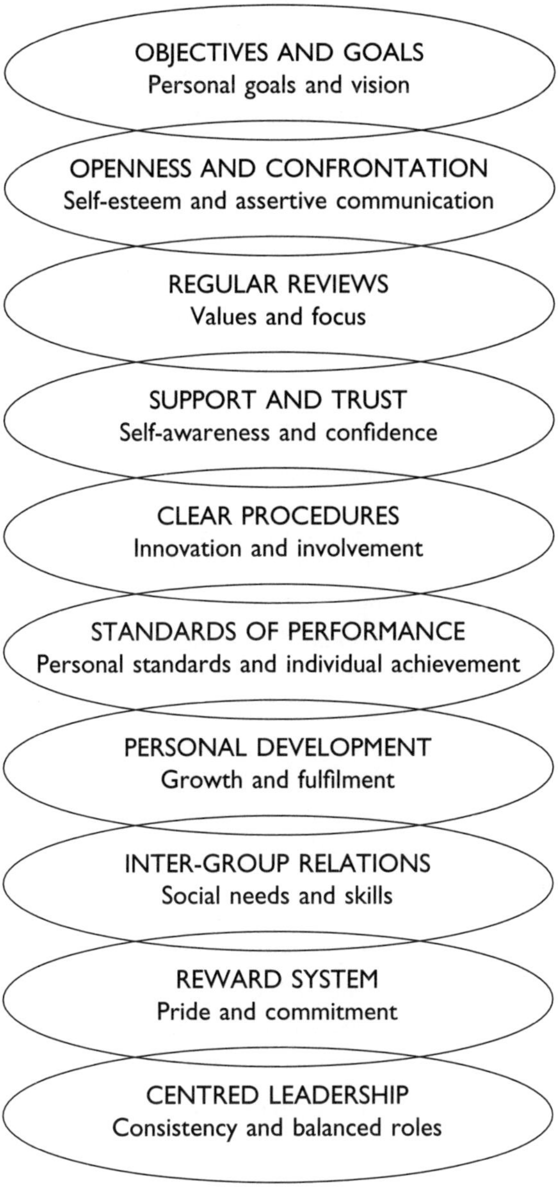

OBJECTIVES AND GOALS
Personal goals and vision

OPENNESS AND CONFRONTATION
Self-esteem and assertive communication

REGULAR REVIEWS
Values and focus

SUPPORT AND TRUST
Self-awareness and confidence

CLEAR PROCEDURES
Innovation and involvement

STANDARDS OF PERFORMANCE
Personal standards and individual achievement

PERSONAL DEVELOPMENT
Growth and fulfilment

INTER-GROUP RELATIONS
Social needs and skills

REWARD SYSTEM
Pride and commitment

CENTRED LEADERSHIP
Consistency and balanced roles

Figure 7.3   The Synergy Chain Process. Copyright © Hilarie Owen

We know that old paradigms die hard – but we also know they contain the seeds of their own transformation. As an individual this presents you with a personal challenge. You are probably a manager in a hierarchy – or a consultant advising organizations. You are someone who is open to ideas and change. What is your initial personal reaction to the idea of moving beyond the hierarchy where there are only a handful of managers? The need for management development will decrease and MBAs could disappear to be replaced with different postgraduate courses containing a more humanities-biased base. The shift requires you and everyone else to personally evaluate their present world of work and organizational power. Transformation is never easy.

To understand the difficulties there is a wonderful story Warren Bennis tells of when he became president of a university.

> My moment of truth came toward the end of my first ten months. It was one of those nights in the office. The clock was moving toward four in the morning, and I was still not through with the incredible mass of paper stacked before me. I was bone weary and soul weary, and I found myself muttering, 'Either I can't manage this place, or it's unmanageable.' I reached for my calendar and ran my eyes down each hour, half hour, quarter hour to see where my time had gone that day, the day before, the month before . . . My discovery was this: I had become the victim of a vast, amorphous, unwitting, unconscious conspiracy to prevent me from doing anything whatever to change the university's status quo.[20]

As long as we stay fixed in the present structures, systems, thinking and behaviour, it will be almost impossible for individuals to express their leadership potential and real change will elude us. The lesson from the above story is that one single person will not change the world, but 10 who grow to 100 who grow to 1000 who grow to 10 000 and so on will. What is being proposed is not a revolution as such. Revolutions are bloody and result in both winners and losers. We know from our history that destructive practices do not work in the long run. In the end the aggressors always destroy themselves, making way for others who know how to cooperate and live together. Life is not so much a competitive struggle for survival than a triumph of cooperation and creativity.

This book is proposing something in line with what Daniel Quinn said: 'To overthrow the hierarchy is pointless; we just want to leave it behind.' What is being offered here is a new model – a new way to build organizations where human ideas, creativity and spirit can act to unleash leadership everywhere. The question is, how do you achieve this? How do you transform organizations and unleash leadership? How do you develop circular network organizations? How do you move from where you are to where you should be?

8

Unleashing Leaders

*Traveller, our time together has begun a graceful yet irreversible
learning process. I have given you these laws not to bind you, but
to free you.*

Dan Millman

To transform organizations and unleash leaders we have to realize
that the process involves both organizational and individual
development *together*. The answer is *not* an organizational development
plan with separate training. The action of company directors is not to
wait and see who else takes this process on board and then decide
whether to follow or learn from the pioneers. Each organization will
have its own journey, with its own learning and outcomes. Neither
should chief executives nor managing directors give leadership
development to the human resource director to oversee, for *all* the top
team are responsible for leadership development as they are indeed for
organizational development too.

Transforming organizations is an evolutionary process of several
stages. However, this does not mean it is necessarily slow. Sometimes
evolution jumps forward fast to what is known as 'intergenerational
learning'. Here the behaviour of the individuals rather than the
environmental change is the driving force. This fast learning occurs
when individuals have the capacity to invent new behaviour and have

a process of transmitting this from individuals to the community at large. Therefore any process we use for unleashing leaders needs to include the ability to learn fast.

To guide us we have a framework that outlines the new memes to address current thinking, behaviour and culture. For the organization the issue is one of structure. Organizational development involves transforming the flatter hierarchy or matrix structure to a circular web or net structure. For the individuals, the challenge is one of behaviour – this includes perception, beliefs, power, control and so on. Therefore the process to use is one that is aligned to the framework and focuses on both organizational development and individual development with the purpose to unleash leadership throughout. Where do we begin?

1: Dialogue

There is only one place to begin and that is with the present situation. Does the organization desire to change its present structure? What is the present behaviour of those in the organization? Those who have benefited most from the present will be the most reluctant and this fact needs to be addressed. There is only one way to begin – through dialogue as conceived by David Bohm. This notion of dialogue is a multifaceted process and goes far beyond conversation and discussion. It is a process that explores the wide range of our existence. Dialogue explores our closely held values, the nature and intensity of our emotions, the patterns of our thought processes, our mental models, our memory, inherited cultural myths and beliefs, the way we structure moment-to-moment experience and how thought is generated at a collective level. The process questions our deeply held assumptions, beliefs, culture, meaning and identity. Finally, it tests our definitions of work, organizations and life.

Dialogue in this situation comes from collaborating with others and learning through different experiences. It often means struggling to understand; building a confidence in a new tomorrow after the scepticism drawn from the past; and coming to terms with the realization that leadership can come from anywhere in the organization.

Throughout the process, dialogue allows participants to recognize their assumptions and views in the hope of developing a new understanding, replacing defensive posturing and a feeling of isolation. This is paramount in the first step of moving toward transformation. It requires all managers and directors to personally evaluate their world and the change in where power lies in the organization. For transformation will spread power and responsibility throughout and control will need to be replaced with trust.

Through dialogue transformation begins: first by learning through the experience of everyone else and facing our own feelings. This learning is experiential or, as Jean Piaget called it, 'learning by accommodation' rather than listening to a trainer and being told what to do or what to understand. Experiential learning comes more from within rather than from the outside world. Second, transformation occurs in behaviour through addressing fears, perceptions and assumptions about ourselves and others. In doing this, we address the issues Argyris found demonstrated in the defensive and denial behaviour identified in earlier chapters when we were looking at the demise of organizations.

Dialogue should continue until there is change, though persuasion is not called for. The process isn't easy and can be frustrating at times as each individual becomes aware of their own reactions and feelings. The focus at the start of the dialogue is on unleashing leadership throughout the organization and the implications of this on its present state.

When change occurs collectively it is very powerful and the opportunity arises to work with others in making the transition to the new. Everyone should be involved in this including those at the top of the present hierarchy. For the future is created by all people with aspirations, values and growing expectations. This process is likely to continue as long as those involved want it to. Once established, step two can be undertaken.

2: Establish purpose

In most organizations the top team sit on top of the hierarchy or matrix. The present scenario is for the top team to develop a vision and 'sell it' to the rest of the organization. The limitation of 'selling' a vision is that employees feel manipulated, don't have ownership and therefore have little commitment to this 'vision'.

Instead the top team need to begin the process by answering the question: what is the purpose of our organization? If the answer they come up with is 'to make money' they have a problem because it does not give meaning and purpose to those who work every day trying to achieve this.

Making money was the answer given to me by a top team recently who were having problems working together and maintaining their business. Their financial performance was declining and profits were dwindling. The focus had been on making money and they were failing. The workforce felt unhappy and divisions were occurring between head office and the rest of the company. Their solution was to bring in a new managing director who everyone hoped would come up with a vision and 'fix' everything. The top team did not take responsibility for what had occurred to date. Until they identify the true purpose of their company they will continue to struggle. We have seen similar scenarios with the rise of dot.com companies.

Purpose is the reason why the organization exists. This should be stated in one sentence. This 'purpose' is then tested at the next stage.

3: Involve everyone in the transformation

We now need to bring everyone into the transformation where the focus is on developing the organization so leadership potential can become a reality. From the new memecomplex framework we see organizations as complete systems, interacting within itself and with its environment. Therefore transformation requires a whole system approach. This idea isn't totally new. Richard Beckard developed a model in the 1960s for planning change in large, complex organizations. He extended this to what he called 'confrontation meetings' which were designed for a group of managers from all levels of the organization to assess the health of the organization and put together action plans to improve things.

The work was taken up and built on by Ronald Lippitt in the 1970s and 1980s. The prime focus of these projects was to change the behaviour of managers from defending their territory to being open, communicating better and working together in a collaborative way with co-workers. The process involved three dimensions: the first was to become better acquainted with the environment; the second was to evaluate the organization's present situation realistically; and the third was to create what Lippitt called 'a preferred future'. Lippitt believed that the big danger in deciding the future was its limiting involvement to a small group – that is, the board – who were deciding the future for the whole organization. For him, this would limit the resources of imagination, experience and energy available to implementing the goals.

The work on large system change is at present based on the formula (D)issatisfaction with the present plus future (V)ision, plus concrete (F)irst steps has to be greater than (I)nertia. During the late 1980s Kathleen Dannemiller took up the work and developed the process with a team in the USA who worked with clients such as Ford Motors and Marriott Hotels.

When the whole system is involved, there is increased information flow, communication, system focus and quick response. The whole system is generating energy with many interpretations, thinking about itself, what it wants to be and how to get there. This does not happen with change programmes based on training sessions for 10 or 12 people at a time. Imagine the energy and ideas coming from 200 or 300 or even 500 people going through a change event *together*. I saw and felt this energy when attending a training programme to learn the process with Kathleen Dannemiller in the USA as we practised with a company. I saw it again with a client in the UK who had every single member of the organization together for three days to work through the change. Back at their head office a couple of people were hired for those three days to take messages. The courage to undertake the wholescale approach paid off and the company have not looked back.

Using wholescale technology, real issues are dealt with and everyone ends up going in the same direction together. People support what they create and today they need to create network organizations in which they work through the issues together. As Margaret Wheatley says:

> Reality emerges from our process of observation, from the decisions we the observers make about what we will see. It does not exist independent of those activities. Therefore we cannot talk people into reality because there truly is no reality to describe if they haven't been there. People can only become aware of the reality of the plan by interacting with it, by creating different possibilities through their personal processes of observation.[1]

Those who feel the most threatened in this are the managers. Peter Senge has a message for managers:

> Learning organizations demand a new view of leadership . . . They [managers] are responsible for building organizations where people continually expand their capabilities to understand complexity, clarify vision, and improve shared mental models . . . There is new work here, and we must be willing to abandon our whole paradigm of who we are as managers to master this new work.[2] Are you and your colleagues willing to do this?

During this step, wholescale technology is used but the formula of D + V + Fs is changed to work with the new memecomplex framework. The new way of understanding organizations and systems thinking is part of this process. The *activity* is focused on everyone in the organization working through the relationships and *values* required to achieve the purpose that the top team will have discussed with the rest of the employees. The fundamental task is to recognize the pattern of the organization that will emerge in the future as it is *this* that will decide the new structure.

Suddenly the realization will dawn on the individuals that the hierarchy is gone and has been replaced with a better structure. This new structure is based on the relationships and interconnections needed to achieve the organization's purpose. Therefore pattern comes first, followed by structure, followed by behaviour. This order is vital and consistent with all living things. At the same time, the structure is aligned with the new memecomplex. Once the structure is agreed the group can decide the right behaviour throughout for leadership to thrive everywhere.

The board are removed from the top of a hierarchy and placed at the centre. Power kept them at the top; trust will keep them at the centre. In the new organization, trust is the new force. The board are more visible at the centre and consistent behaviour that matches their language will build trust. Their role includes reaching out in the network and communicating far more. Everyone in the organization watches the behaviour of directors, which they decide whether to believe and follow. Individuals always decide whom they are going to follow and how to express their own leadership. This truth must be recognized.

At the wholescale event, some of the implications are worked through and teams are formed. Resistance to the change is low because everyone has participated while energy and creativity are captured. During the process individuals are able to express their leadership and learn from it.

Together a shared vision is developed. The danger is not following through after the event. Therefore focus now moves to the behaviour and thinking needed for day-to-day work in the new organization. Actions must be followed through. The need now is to develop teams and individual leadership. My experience is that the best way seems to be to actually begin with team development. I believe this is because a team learns quicker and has a goal to achieve. It means that at this stage of development individuals can focus on a real issue or goal as well as addressing their own personal goals. Within no time the team members relax and issues such as openness, trust, standards of behaviour and performance and so on can be addressed.

4: Teams or clusters

Team development using Owen's synergy chain process (Figure 7.3) will enhance the performance and behaviour of teams. The model was developed following two years of research with the RAF Red Arrows when I set out to find how to develop a world-class team even though team members may change. Previous theories on teams didn't go far enough in developing outstanding performance and creating the *esprit de corps* required for teams to thrive.

The model contains two chains that when put together create synergy – greater effect than the individual performance of the team members. The diagnostic measuring tools and programme resulting from this have been used with teams throughout Europe, the USA and Middle East. Everywhere performance is enhanced and the team is strong. In recent years the programme has worked with global teams where members from different nationalities work together for a common purpose. The programme ensures that the diversity in the team is used positively rather than becoming a source of discontent.

The success of these teams and how they move around and connect with others will be paramount. If a team member reverts back to 'old' behaviour, other team members are responsible for dealing with the situation and ensuring high standards are maintained in all.

5: Individual leadership development

Leadership development should also focus on the individual. Rather than complying to a set of general competencies, each individual will express their leadership differently as a result of knowing who they are. This internalizing and understanding is crucial to learning and personal mastery. When individuals understand themselves, know who they are and what they want through reflection away from the workplace they can begin to become leaders. Over the years when I have included this process with people while working on developing their leadership, it has always had the greatest impact and longest lasting effect on them as individuals. They are given a notebook with a series of questions to answer. Each individual goes to a place or room alone and works through the questions. In the quiet they begin an internal journey.

When developing leadership the words of Galileo are worth remembering: 'We cannot teach people anything; we can only help them discover it.' What they should be discovering is their self-knowledge, how open they are to feedback and learning from all experiences, how they impact on people, how connected they are to everyone and everything around them and finally how to develop their ability to teach and mentor others while always learning themselves. Leadership is a lifetime's endeavour and the classroom is life itself. Some are better pupils than others while many need support and help.

Team and leadership development is for *all*, including the directors who should live the new behaviour for others to see. This is far stronger than 'selling' a vision because the board are now *living* the vision. This takes us to other options in the process of unleashing leaders.

Role models

One observation I have made in identifying how people 'learn' their leadership is that many people gain a great deal through hearing the stories of other leaders. A broad range of 'speakers' or storytellers can be incorporated into any leadership development. To get maximum benefit from this, encourage people to have specific questions for the speakers and have a 'dialogue' following the talk. Get as many people as possible to 'tell their stories'. These stories are powerful affirmations of the human spirit and leadership. They touch us and we realize each one of us has a leadership journey.

Action learning

To maximize learning and behaviour changes, and address the issues affecting everyone, this option includes developing action learning sets around the organization. These leadership sets focus specifically on real issues, develop creative processes and utilize the knowledge inside the brains of all. The action learning sets develop leadership while resolving real issues and putting into the place the necessary actions for the new structure to succeed. At the same time they encourage a holistic approach and support for others in resolving their issues.

During this stage, individuals are beginning to realize their leadership capabilities as the sets work through specific leadership issues. Leadership skills are brought out as and when they are needed. Participants have found this far more effective than 'classroom type training' as it is dealing with the things that are important to the participants and it enables them to reflect away from the busy workplace.

6: Coaching and mentoring

Ongoing coaching and mentoring should be available for everyone including directors. A frequent problem with this form of development is one of clarification. What is the difference between coaching and mentoring? Who should be a coach or mentor? Should the focus be on work performance? What if the problem is more personal? Who is the client? How confidential is confidentiality?

Although coaching is for everyone, the truth is that not everyone can be a coach or wants to be. A coach should focus on the individual or team with the aim of improving performance. They may not be an 'expert' in the work of the individual or team; their expertise is drawing out the best in others. If the issue becomes one of a more personal nature, the coach should only look at it from the viewpoint of how it is affecting the performance of the individual at work. A good coach also knows when to recommend someone else to help resolve a personal issue. Confidentiality remains with the individual being coached. If it is a serious matter the coach can try to encourage the individual to inform someone in the organization or speak to someone in the organization on their behalf and with the individual's permission.

A mentor is usually more experienced than the individual in sharing knowledge and encouragement. The mentoring process involves coaching, advising, career guidance and counselling. The mentor cares about the individual and acts as a guide.

In both situations the important part is in matching the two people. Coaching and mentoring are expensive because of their long-term commitment. Therefore an organization needs to be clear they are seeing the benefits of improved performance and behaviour. At the same time individuals need to clarify with their coach or mentor their objectives at the first meeting and to make assessments on the basis of achieving them.

7: Review and evaluation

Review and evaluation is an ongoing action. It is important to be clear about the aim of this transformation, and to review progress. What is the outcome? The end result is an environment where leadership is totally unleashed within the organization and expressed fully. How do we recognize this? It is recognizable when individuals throughout the organization:

- give themselves permission to challenge the status quo
- are actively encouraged to question 'the way things are done around here'
- take risks and fail occasionally and are rewarded for it
- stretch themselves and can look back at how much new knowledge and skill they have acquired
- spend time networking throughout the organization to find out what needs to be done and who needs to be involved to make it happen
- are skilled in sharing knowledge, problem solving, decision-making and risk assessment
- participate fully in workplace and project-based teams
- have fun and enjoy coming to work
- know who they are, what makes them unique, and
- are comfortable expressing their leadership for a worthwhile purpose.

A model of this process (Figure 8.1) shows how each part is interlinked and connected, providing a solution to both organization and individual

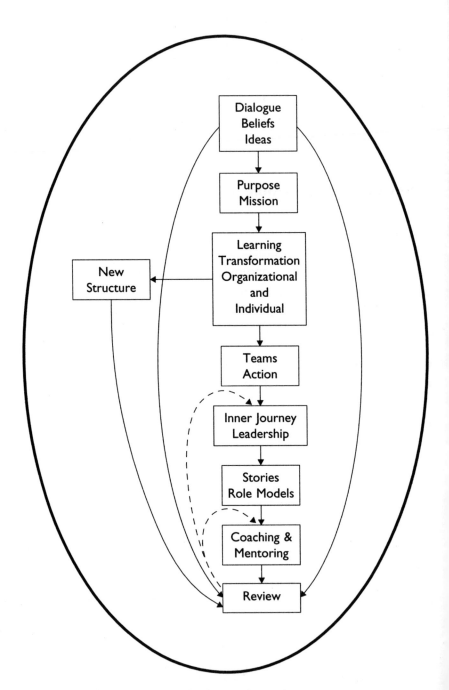

Figure 8.1   Unleashing Leaders in Organizations

development. The solution is also tied to the memecomplex framework creating a work community in a circular structure where knowledge, self-regulation, purpose and meaning, learning, creativity, flexibility, diversity, self-actualization and generating energy are normal parts of the behaviour. Everyone is connected and interconnected in teams with suppliers and customers. Chaos and change is no longer a problem as the organization can adapt and the directors focus on the whole, not different parts.

The value of this model and process is its wholeness. If an organization takes one or two of these steps the result is limited. Together, as an interconnected whole, the process will enable true transformation and leadership throughout. Through changing the shape of our organization we can begin to change the behaviour and thinking within them.

Conclusion: From Homo Sapiens to Homo Proteus (Shape Changer Being)

All this world is heavy with the promise of greater things, and a day will come, one day in the unending succession of days, when beings who are now latent in our loins shall stand upon this earth as one stands upon a footstool and shall touch the stars.

H. G. Wells

Leadership is not mystical or rare. Leadership is not a part of management that can be bolted on. Leadership is the individual expression of the human spirit and as such requires opportunity and environment to be expressed, practised and valued. If we require leadership from everyone in an organization it is not sufficient to achieve this through training. The hierarchical structure – though flatter and more matrix with its rigid processes, management and culture – will always confine leadership. It is interesting that in the armed forces during peacetime management rules. In a war zone situation one of the first things to disappear is the structured hierarchy and leadership appears. For the rest, many people never 'discover' who they are as a leader and so leadership appears to us as something 'special'.

Today the world has changed and continues to transform and with it our knowledge and understanding of how it works. Organizations have also changed but true transformation is only beginning. As human beings we have to learn to become shape changers. Our minds hold us back for there are still many beliefs from our distant past to overcome.

Our visit to ancient civilizations showed us the clue to what has to change. In Ancient Egypt, Greece and Rome, new conquerors eventually took over but they were just the opportunists. The real failing of these civilizations was that as time passed each made the same mistake – they became static. Sons did what fathers did and daughters did what mothers did. In doing so their human potential was limited and more so, the freedom of their imagination in what could be. Whether belief or religion or politics, dogma took control and the freedom to think differently came too late. Those who have questioned the 'order' – such as Socrates, Jesus, Galileo, Sir Thomas More and many others – paid with their lives. The fundamental core to their being was integrity, truth and ethics. Without these leadership will become yet another 'management fad'. A system of values and new structures is necessary for humans to express their leadership. Egypt, Greece and Rome failed under the power and politics of people without values. The post-cold-war era is in danger of repeating that failure with power, politics and business low in values.

Today individuals have knowledge but this knowledge must be used to create our future as well as deal with day-to-day matters. The knowledge required is threefold: first self-knowledge, which we gain from experience, physical exercise, reflection and learning, our history and philosophy; second the knowledge we gain from the experience of the arts and culture; and finally, the explanation and understanding of our world from scientists among whom are ecologists and biologists. It is the accumulation of intellect, emotion, imagination and humour that enables us to be fully human beings. These are what should be taught in schools and in our libraries. These are what should be taught in lifelong learning. As long as the majority sit back in ignorance, believing old beliefs and letting others run the world we will continue to repeat what previous civilizations have done.

Leadership must be expressed by the many instead of the few. With leadership comes responsibility and integrity in who and what we are as human beings. This is the message within both *In Search of Leaders* and *Unleashing Leaders*. Here the focus has been on our organizations.

In the quest to unleash leadership throughout I propose that both individuals and organizations can now transform through learning and development. This new synthesis of human and organization developing together is possible when we work with a framework that we call a memecomplex where the evolutionary process has at its heart the freedom to become the leaders we are all capable of becoming no matter how small or great.

Earlier in the book we saw the decay occurring in organizations caused by the few who withhold information, behave with arrogance and self-interest, make themselves rich and betray the public or customers. The hierarchy as a structure enables this to happen. For some the argument is that entropy is a natural occurrence and that some organizations will disappear while others will be launched. The truth is that the second law of thermodynamics states that entropy – disorder – in any system will increase over time *unless energy is added to the system*. This energy is not sufficient through change initiatives such as total quality management (TQM), business process re-engineering (BPR) or downsizing; the true energy comes from transformation of one state to another.

Max Plank who discovered this law stated that the two states must be characterized and known for transformation to occur. Until this point most organizations have only known the hierarchical state, whether flat or otherwise. Now with a framework to guide us and a process for learning and transforming as individuals and organizations, it is possible to create a new structure that is circular, flexible, has power distributed, allows diversity, can adjust quickly to its environment and unleash leadership throughout. This new architecture with its new values and behaviours will provide the energy to the system to stop the entropy.

Leadership cannot be expressed in a rigid, fixed structure – leadership needs a fluid, dynamic structure. All knowledge and information must flow throughout to enable learning in the new structure. Learning is the reason for acquiring knowledge. However, knowledge is more than facts. Our understanding of the world, particularly during the twentieth century, came more from imagination than rigour. It is this creative energy that is needed in organizations today; whether in the private or public sector, whether business or politics. To achieve creative energy we need to unleash leaders everywhere and the best way is to develop both the individuals and the organization together. The reason organizations should unleash leaders throughout is to set free the creative energy and the human spirit that for too long have been suppressed by structure. In the process of changing the shape of all organizations and unleashing leaders everywhere we can identify the best pattern, the best structure and the best behaviour to achieve the purpose of the organization.

The biggest untruth in the world today is that many believe their organizations have already transformed and that there is nothing new in the message here. Very, very few have transformed to what is required. The old memes are strong and when threatened will fight to stay in the minds of people. The words of David Bohm describe this brilliantly when he said: 'If you have fish in a tank and you put a glass barrier in there, the fish keep away from it. And then if you take away the glass barrier they never cross the barrier and they think the whole world is that.'[1]

There is a whole world beyond the glass barrier of hierarchical organizations and management. Unleash the leaders in your organization and the creative energy that is required in the world today will express itself through the leadership of the many. Yes, it is frightening – we are all afraid. Yet our past can teach us that the human spirit can achieve what it set out to do when the will is able.

This book can only touch the surface of what is a huge task ahead. With its sister book *In Search of Leaders*, the aim has been to try and understand leadership and how to develop leaders throughout organizations. To carry on the work a body of people who are committed to developing leadership in the world has come together.

The Institute of Leadership was launched in May 2000 and has members joining every day. The work undertaken at the Institute includes research and developing a knowledge gateway for leadership. Fundamental to its work is to take the ideas in the two books and work with organizations to help them transform. The Leadership Quest is a 12-month, innovative, experiential programme for individuals who want to discover their leadership potential. It is based on the circular journey outlined in *In Search of Leaders*. Proteus is the consultancy arm of the Institute, dealing with the transformation of organizations with the specific purpose of unleashing leaders. Our web site is www.iofl.org or contact me at hilarie.owen@iofl.org

Final words

The world is transforming with the sole purpose of bringing about true individual freedom in every walk of life. It is as Hegel wrote: 'The history of the world is none other than the progress of the consciousness of freedom.'[2] Part of this freedom is expressed in leadership and is the reason for its pursuit at this time in a transforming world. When we unleash leaders we are simply following the inevitable unfolding of human evolution. We are moving forward in the progress of humankind and human consciousness. There is no map to show us the way but it is hoped these two books together can be part of the compass to point us in the right direction.

At a recent book-signing event I was surprised and pleased to see a familiar face. 'What are you doing here, Herbert?' I asked.

He smiled and said, 'I wondered if you had time for another trip – perhaps into the future this time?'

'Will I like what I see and what we have become?' I asked.

Herbert looked at me and replied: 'When are you going to trust the universe and realize that everything is for us to learn and become the best we can be? You know you have to believe and live what you write. That is the hardest task of all. But will it help if I tell you that we humans do eventually "get it"?'

So off we went and as I approached the time machine I remembered the words of William Blake:

To see a World in a Grain of Sand
And a Heaven in a Wild Flower
Hold Infinity in the palm of your hand
And Eternity in an hour.[3]

References

Chapter 1

1. Jay Conger and Beth Benjamin, *Building Leaders*, Jossey Bass, San Francisco, CA, 1999
2. Ibid.
3. Ibid.
4. Letter from civil servant in Department of Education and Employment to author, discussing leadership.
5. Part of *Human Resource Strategy*, American Express UK in 1989/9
6. Noel Tichy, *The Leadership Engine*, HarperCollins, New York, 1997

Chapter 2

1. Alvin and Heidi Tofler, *New York Times*, 31 October 1993
2. Department of Industry Report, 'Differences in companies' performance', November 1997
3. Ibid.
4. McKinsey research into UK company performance, taken from article in *Financial Times*, 15 May 1998
5. Report from *Economist* Intelligence Unit, 'Productivity in motor industry in Europe', 8 June 1998
6. Alan Briskin, *The Stirring of the Soul in the Workplace*, Berrett-Koehler, San Francisco, CA, 1998
7. Institute of Management and UMIST survey 1999
8. Ibid.

9.   American Management Association and Wyatt Consultants
10. Alan Briskin, op. cit.
11. David Birchall and Laurence Lyons, *Creating Tomorrow's Organization*, Pitmans, London, 1995
12. Institute of Directors/Bathwick Group Survey reported in *Financial Times*, 27 January 1998
13. Ibid.
14. Ibid.
15. Small Business Research Trust, Lloyds TSB
16. Industrial Society and Resource Connection study, 'Flexible Working and male professionals: Can't change, won't change', 2000
17. Harvard Business School, 'Study of Harvard Alumni', 1997
18. Catalyst, New York, 'Study of Female Entrepreneurs', 1997
19. *London Business School Global Entrepreneur Monitor*, sponsored by Apex Partners, June 1999
20. Lloyds TSB Bank, 'Gender No Barrier to Research', 24 February 1999
21. 'DM 2015 Immersive Scenarios', Dept of Trade and Industry, 1999
22. *The 1997 Ashridge Management Index*, Ashridge Research, Ashridge, Berkhamstead, Herts, England
23. Richard Koch and Ian Godden, *Managing without Management*, Nicholas Brealey, 1997
24. Ibid.
25. David Taylor, Association of IT Directors, quoted in the *Independent*, 6 September 1999
26. Koch and Godden, op. cit.
27. Abraham Zaleznik, *The Managerial Mystique*, Harper & Row, New York, 1989
28. *Economist* Intelligence Unit/Hewett Associates report, 'Building and Retaining Global Talent Towards 2002', 1998
29. Ibid.
30. Cary Cooper, 'Bullying in the UK', TUC/CBI-sponsored report, UMIST, 1999
31. Robert Heller quoted in Koch and Godden, op. cit.
32. Koch and Godden, op. cit.

Chapter 3

1.   FSA statement on mis-selling pensions, reported in the *Guardian*, 9 August 1998.
2.   Margaret Thatcher

3. Robert Winnett and Kathryn Cooper, Study of 50 companies, *Sunday Times*, 16 July 2000

4. Consumer Association Report, 'Top 20 Mortgage Scams', 2000

5. Don Cruickshank, 'Report on Banks and Building Societies', March 2000

6. Terry Burke, 'University of Westminster Survey for the Cooperative Bank', 1993

7. Arthur Anderson, 'New York report on ethical codes of conduct in US companies 1999', *Financial Times*, 19 August 1999

8. Cadbury Report, May 1992. Established by the accountancy profession: chairman Sir Adrian Cadbury, former chairman of Cadbury Schweppes

9. J. Dahya, A.A. Lonie and D.M. Power 'Corporate Governance', Dundee University, April 1996

10. Greenbury Report, July 1995. Established by CBI; chairman Sir Richard Greenbury, former chairman of Marks and Spencer

11. Hampel Report, August 1997. Formed to monitor Cadbury and Greenbury Codes; chaired by Sir Ronnie Hampel, chairman ICI

12. Ibid.

13. Chancellor Gordon Brown, quoted in the *Guardian*, 22 July 1998

14. SCA Consulting, as reported in the *Sunday Times*, 9 August 1998

15. PricewaterhouseCoopers, 'Pay and Performance', 1999

16. Peter Oppenheimer, *Management Today*, July 1999

17. President Clinton at a business breakfast in 1998

18. Vic Coleman, Chief Inspector for Railways, 'Health and Safety Executive Report on Railtrack', 1999

19. Daniel Quinn, *Beyond Civilization*, Harmony Books, Random House, 1999

20. Audit Commission Report, 'Protecting the Public Purse', published 1 December 1999

21. Government review, 'Early Retirement in the Public Sector', 1999

22. Anne Coote, in the *Guardian*, 11 May 1999

23. Alexandra Harney, in the *Financial Times*, 10 July 2000

24. *Independent*, 15 March 2000

25. Ibid.

26. *Economist*, 20–26 June 1998

27. Report on European Commission, 1999

28. Ibid.

29. Ibid.

30. Koch and Godden, op. cit.

31. Article on International Olympic Committee in *New York* Magazine, 1 March 1999

32. Reported in the *Guardian*, 30 July 1999

33. House of Commons Report on Royal Opera House 1997

34. Ibid.

35. Ibid.

36. Ibid.
37. Lawrence Report by Sir William MacPherson, February 1999
38. Corruption Preventing Strategy launched by Police Summer 2000
39. *Legal Week*, August 1999
40. Ibid.
41. Report by Sir David Ramsbothom, Chief Inspector of Prisons, 18 December 1999
42. Ashworth Report, January 1999
43. Ibid.
44. Franks Report, 'British Business Schools', British Institute of Management, 1963
45. Mant Report, 'The Experienced Manager – A Major Resource', British Institute of Management, 1969
46. Owen Report, 'Business Schools Programmes – The Requirements of British Manufacturing Industry', the Council of Industry for Management Education and British Institute of Management, 1970
47. Coopers and Lybrand/Manpower Services Commission/National Economic Development Office report, 'A Challenge to Complacency', November 1985
48. 'Management Training – Context and Practice', School of Management, University of Bath, June 1986
49. Manpower Services Commission, National Economic Development Council and British Institute of Management, 'The Making of Managers', Charles Handy, April 1987; British Institute of Managers and CBI, 'The making of British Managers', John Constable and Roger McCormick, April 1987
50. Koch and Godden, op. cit.
51. Booz, *Ways Managers Spend Time*, Allan & Hamilton
52. John Kotter, *Leading Change*, Harvard Business School Press, 1996
53. Koch and Godden, op. cit.
54. Tom Peters, *Liberation Management*, 1992
55. Birchall and Lyons, op. cit.
56. Vaclav Havel acceptance speech for the Philadelphia Liberty Medal at the Independence Hall Speech, 4 July 1994
57. Laura Berman Fortgang, speaking at the Third Annual Coaching and Mentoring Conference, Europe 2000 for Linkage International, 4 July 2000

Chapter 4

1. Queen Elizabeth I at Tilbury before the Armada on 9 August 1588. Extract from Brian MacArthur (ed.), *The Penguin Book of Historic Speeches*, Penguin, 1996

2. Extract from the Speos Artemidos inscription of King Hatchepsut, translated by A. Gardiner, 'The Great Speos Artemidos Inscription', *Journal of Egyptian Archeology* 32: 43–56, 1946
3. Aristotle, 'Politics', in Claude Orrieux and Pauline Schmitt Pantell, *A History of Ancient Greece*, Blackwell, Oxford, 1999
4. Jean-Pierre Vernant et al., *The Greeks*, translation by Charles Lambert and Teresa Lavender, Fagan, Chicago, 1995
5. Robert Fritz, *Corporate Tides*, Berrett-Koehler, San Francisco, 1996
6. Abraham Maslow, *Maslow on Management*, John Wiley & Sons, New York, 1998

Chapter 5

1. Ibid.
2. Richard Dawkins, *The Selfish Gene*, Oxford University Press, 1976
3. Ibid.
4. Ibid.

Chapter 6

1. Thomas Kuhn, *The Structure of Scientific Revolutions*, University of Chicago Press, Chicago, 1962
2. Fritjof Capra, *The Web of Life*, HarperCollins, New York, 1997
3. Abraham Maslow, *Maslow on Management*, John Wiley & Sons, New York, 1998
4. Werner Heisenberg, *Physics and Beyond*, Harper Row, New York, 1971
5. Ludwig von Bertalanffy, *General Systems Theory*, Braziller, New York, 1968
6. Marilyn Ferguson, *The Aquarian Conspiracy*, Granada, 1982
7. James Gleick, *Chaos*, Heinemann, 1988
8. Ibid.
9. Quoted in Gleick, op. cit.
10. Ibid.
11. Quoted in Capra, op. cit.
12. Arie de Geus, *The Living Company*, Nicholas Brealey, London, 1999
13. Quoted in Capra, op. cit.
14. Ibid.
15. James Lovelock, *Healing Gaia*, Harmony Books, New York, 1991
16. Capra, op. cit.

17. Quoted in Capra, op. cit.
18. David Bohm, *Unfolding Meaning*, Routledge, London, 1985
19. Eric Trist, 'A Social-Technical Critique of Scientific Management', in E. Trist and H. Murray (eds.), *The Social Engagement of Social Science*, volume 2, University of Pennsylvania Press, 1993
20. Ibid.
21. Maslow, op. cit.
22. Ibid.

Chapter 7

1. David Birchall and Laurence Lyons, *Creating Tomorrow's Organization*, Pitmans, London, 1995
2. Gareth Morgan, *Creative Organization Theory*, Sage Publications, California, 1989
3. Lee Sproull and Sara Kiesler, *Connections – New Ways of Working in the Networked Organization*, MIT Press, Massachusetts, 1991
4. Sally Helgesen, *Web of Inclusion*, Doubleday, New York, 1995
5. Ibid.
6. ˙ Ibid.
7. Erich Jantsch, *The Self Organizing Universe*, Pergamon Press, Oxford, 1980
8. Tom Peters, *Thriving on Chaos*, MacMillan, London, 1988
9. Peter Senge, *The Fifth Discipline*, Century Business, 1992
10. Jean Piaget, *The Psychology of Intelligence*, Routledge and Kegan Paul, London, 1986
11. Discussed in Senge, op. cit.
12. Arie de Geus, *The Living Company*, Nicholas Brealey, London, 1999
13. Thomas Stewart, *Intellectual Capital*, Nicholas Brealey, London, 1997
14. Helgesen, op. cit.
15. Ibid.
16. Senge, op. cit.
17. Capra, op. cit.
18. Hilarie Owen, *Top Flight Teams*, Kogan Page, 1996
19. Marilyn Ferguson, *The Aquarian Conspiracy*, Granada, 1982
20. Quoted in Peters, op. cit.
21. Daniel Quinn, *Beyond Civilization*, Crown, New York, 1999

Chapter 8

1. Margaret Wheatley, *Leadership and the New Science*, Berrett-Koehler, San Francisco, 1994
2. Ibid.

Conclusion

1. David Bohm, quoted in John Horgan, *The End of Science*, Little Brown and Company, London, 1997
2. Stephen Houlgate (ed.), *The Hegel Reader*, Blackwell, Oxford, 1998
3. William Blake, 'Auguries of Innocence' *Everyman's Poetry*, Orion Publishing Group, London, 1996

Index

accommodation, learning by 123, 137
accountability
  increase in 37–8
  public sector 25
action learning 143–4
adaptation 103
administration
  ancient Greece 79
  ancient Rome 82
  political 84
Argyris, Chris 123–4
Aristotle 76–7, 119
assimilation, learning by 123

banks, abuse of position 31–2
Beckard, Richard 138
behaviour 103, 114
  change in 128–9, 137
beliefs 123, 127
Bennis, Warren 132
blame culture 39
blockages 8, 121
boards
  arrogance 54
  reform 33–5
  removal 141

Bohm, David vii, 93, 106, 136, 152
Bohr, Neils ix
Briskin, Alan 15, 16
Built to Last scenario 23
bullying 27
bureaucracy 116
  see also hierarchy
business ethics 32–3, 35
business organizations 13–25, 85–6
  change 15–16
  hierarchical structure 4, 5, 13,
    21
  initiatives 24
  internal demands 24–5
  learning 18–19
  productivity 14–15
  restructuring 16–17
  scenarios 23
butterfly effect 99

Cadbury, Sir Adrian 33
Capra, Fritjof 94, 103, 128–9
case studies
  computer company 8–10
  Far East 43–7
  small business 20–2

change vii, 15–16, 86, 88
  behaviour 128–9
  need for 94
  paradigm 93–109
  resistance to 106, 123, 124,
    130–3
  see also transformation
chaos theory 99–100, 110
Chief Executives 38
circular structure 101–2, 110,
    116–17, 136, 147
  alternative to hierarchy 119–20
civil service 5
civilizations 66–9, 150
  collapse 72, 88
  Egyptian 69–74
  Greek 74–81
  Inca 88
  Roman 81–4
coaching 8, 144–5
cognitive systems 102
collaboration 136, 139
collective conscience, Egyptians
    72–3
command economy, Russia 47
commercial interests, football 51–2
communication, networks 117
community 104, 105, 126, 129–30
compensation culture 40, 55
competency model 3–4
completion, Aristotle 77
compliance 3, 6, 7, 16
conformity 16
Conger, Jay 1, 4
control 16–17, 26–7
  collapse of 74
  resources 37
cooperation 104
coping strategy 19–20
corporate . . .
  anorexia 14
  responsibility 36–7
  values 8–10

corruption
  European Parliament 50
  Japan 42
  medical profession 57–8
  police force 55–7
  prevention 49–50, 56–7
  sport 50–2
cost cutting 14, 26
costs, business 22
Crawford, Philip 18
creativity 74, 98, 151–2
Cruickshank, Don 32
culture
  collective 54
  differences 6–7
  propagation 87–91
  and structure 114–15
  see also management mindset;
    memes
customers 115–16
  service to 118
cybernetics 97–8

D+V+F formula 139, 140
Daewoo, restructuring 46
daimon-soul, ancient Greece 80
Dannemiller, Kathleen 139
Dawkins, Richard 87
de Geus, Arie 101, 125
democracy 75–6
demos (citizens), Greece 75–6
development
  leaders 1–10
  organizations vii, viii
  see also evolution
dialogue 136–7
directors, remuneration 34–6,
    37
disassociation 19–20
diversity 105, 129
dogma 150
downsizing xiii, 16–17

e revolution 22, 23
early retirement culture 39–40
ecology 101–6, 110
    links 129–30
economic crisis, Japan 42–3
economic restructuring, South Korea
    46–7
ecosystems 104–5, 129
education, ancient Greece 78
Egyptian civilization 69–74
    freedom of women 70–2
    hierarchy 69–70, 73
    religion 72–3
    river environment 69
Einstein, Albert viii, 95
employees, types 19
enablement ix
energy 139, 151, 152
entrepreneurs, support 22–3
entropy 151
epistemology 127
ethics
    committee 49–50
    programme 32–3
European Commission, fraud 48–9,
    50
evaluation 145–7
evolution
    organizations 66–8, 103–4
    theory of 103
experiential learning 7, 8, 123,
    137

Far East, financial crisis 43–7
Ferguson, Marilyn 97, 130
Feynman, Richard 65
financial crisis, Far East 43–7
fluidity 151
football
    outdated attitudes 52
    self-interest 51–2
    sex discrimination 52

forward thinking 64
fraud
    European Commission 48–9, 50
    public sector 39
    see also corruption
Fuller, Buckminster 113

Gaia theory 102, 103
gender issues 40–1
    see also sex discrimination;
        women
glass ceiling 21
Gleick, James 99, 100
global corporations 21, 23
    costs 22
globalization 13, 62–3
goals 9, 131
Goldsmith, James Sir 30, 31
Greek civilization 74–81
    administration 79
    democracy 75–6
    education 78
    hierarchy 78, 119
    slaves 76–7
    spiritual gap 79–80
    women 77–8
Greenbury, Sir Richard 34

Hamel, Gary 14
Hampel, Sir Ronnie 34
harassment, lawyers 58
Hatchepsut (Egyptian queen) 71
Havel, Vaclav 64
Hegel, Georg 153
Hegelsen, Sally 118–19, 126–7
hierarchy 4, 5, 13, 21, 125
    alternatives to 115, 116, 119–20,
        140
    collapse 73–4
    Egyptian civilization 69–70, 73
    Greek civilization 78

hierarchy (*cont.*)
  growth 85–6
  reasons for 87–9
  rejection of 88–9
  Roman civilization 83
  self-interest 50
holistic view 6, 94, 97, 144
human community 104, 105, 126,
  129–30
Hypatia (Roman teacher) 83

IMF *see* International Monetary
  Fund
Inca civilization 88
incompetence
  lawyers 58
  medical profession 57
  Metropolitan Police 54–5
  prison service 59
  special hospitals 59
individuals
  coaching and mentoring
    144–5
  development 107
  energy 80
  leadership 142–4
  potential 12
  transformation 151
industry, origins 85
information era 98, 106
initiatives 24
inner knowledge 96, 122
insider trading 31
Institute of Leadership 152–3
integrity 150
intergenerational learning 135–6
internal demands 24–5
International Monetary Fund (IMF),
  reforms 45–6
International Olympic Committee,
  corruption 50–1
Internet 23

intimidation, prison service 59
involvement 138–41

Japan
  economic crisis 42–3
  organizations 42
  shareholder power 42–3
Jung, Carl 107–8

knowledge 96, 126–7, 150, 151
  inner 96, 122
  knowing 127–8
  revolution in 95
Kuhn, Thomas 93–4

language 105, 129
lawyers, incompetence 58
leaders, role models 143
leadership
  barriers to 49
  development 3, 6–8, 142–4
  gift of vii–viii
  model 145–7
  skills 8
  teaching 7–8
  training 1–3, 4–5
learning xv, 18–19, 121–4, 151
  accommodation 123, 137
  action learning 143–4
  assimilation 123
  experiential 137
  inner knowledge 96, 122
  intergenerational 135–6
  on the job 5–6
  loops 124
  mental models 121
  processes 122–4
  resistance to 124
limited liability, managers 85–6
Lippitt, Ronald 139

living systems 104–5, 129
Lovelock, James 102, 103

management
  blame 25
  current issues 61–2
  failure 30
  growth 59–61
  inadequacy 53–4
  obsolete thinking 28
  constraints on output 14–15
  training 59–61
  vested interest 49
management mindset 7, 28, 54
  public sector 55, 57, 59, 63
managers
  growth 59–61
  limited liability 85–6
  mediocrity 25–8
  procedures 27–8
  transformation 139, 140
Manchester United 51
market economy 30
Maslow, Abraham 86, 94, 108, 109, 130
matrix structure 115, 116
Maturana, Humberto 101–2, 103, 114
MBAs 1
mechanistic view 94, 96, 98, 106
medical profession, scandals 57–8
memecomplex 90–1, 109, 112, 140, 141
memes 87–9, 123, 152
  dynamics of 89–91
  historical 119
  new 93–4, 102, 105
  origin 90
  protection 91
mental models 121

mentoring 4, 8, 144–5
mergers and acquisitions 114
Merseyside Police, corruption 56
Metropolitan Police
  corruption 55–6
  incompetence 54–5
military power, ancient Rome 83
Millman, Dan 135
mis-selling
  mortgages 31–2
  pensions 29–30
mismanagement, Royal Opera House 52–4
Mitsubishi Motors 42
model 145–7
mortgages, mis-selling 32

National Health Service 4
Neanderthals 66–7
nervous system 101–2
network structure 96
  circular 101–2, 110, 115–17, 119–20
  communication 117
  implications 118–20
  knowledge 126–7
  matrix 115, 116
  teams 128
Newton, Sir Isaac 95–6

order see control
organizations
  behaviour 103, 114, 117–18
  business 13–25
  diversity 105
  evolution 66–8, 102, 103–4
  issues 11–12
  Japan 42–3
  learning 121
  measurement 125
  modern 85–91
  new models 94–5, 113–33
  operation of 102

organizations (*cont.*)
  pattern 97–8, 125
  problems 11–28
  purpose 137–8
  structure 97–8, 103, 113–15
  symbiosis 104
  transformation viii, 12–13,
     135–41, 149, 151
out-of-date theory 5
outdated attitudes 52, 63
  see also management mindset

Pamfilova, Ella 47–8
Pandora 78
paradigm shift 93–109, 132
  chaos theory 99–100
  ecology 101–6
  quantum theory 95–6
  social science 107–9
  systems thinking 97–8
pattern 97–8, 125
pension funds 30–1
pensions, mis-selling 29–30
performance 35–6, 131
  directors 34–5, 37
personal growth 9, 118, 131
personality 107–8
Plank, Max 151
police force
  compensation culture 40, 55
  corruption 55–7
  incompetence 54–5
political administration 84
position, and leadership 4–5,
     73–4
possessions 90–1
power
  Roman Empire 83
  shift 118
prehistory 66–7
prison service, incompetence
     59
productivity 14–15, 16

profit, trust v 29–30
profitability 32, 138
psychology 107–9
public sector
  accountability 25
  corruption 55–8
  early retirement 39–40
  fraud 39
  growth 86
  leadership training 4–5
purpose 137–8
Putin, Vladimir 47, 48

quantum physics 95–6, 110
Quinn, Daniel 38, 133

racism
  police force 54–5
  prison service 59
raiders 30–1
Railtrack 37
re-engineering 24
reactive behaviour 17
reality 95–6, 140
reform, boards 33–5
relativity theory 95
religion
  Egyptians 72–3
  Greeks 79–80
remuneration, directors 34–6, 37
resistance to change 106, 123, 124,
     130–3
responsibility 9, 150
  absence of 48–9
  corporate 36–7
  social 31
restructuring xiii, 16–17
retirement 39–40
review 145–7
revitalization 28
role models 143

Roman civilization 81–4
  administration 82
  hierarchy 83
  marriage 81
  Senate 83–4
  slaves 82–3
  work 81–2
Royal Opera House, mismanagement
  52–4
Russia 47–8

scenarios, business organizations 23
self-. . .
  actualization 108, 109, 111
  discipline, Egyptians 73
  employment 21
  expression 149, 152
  interest 37–8, 50, 80, 84
    football clubs 51–2
    police force 56
  knowledge 143, 150
  regulation 97, 102
Senate, ancient Rome 83–4
Senge, Peter 102, 121, 122, 127,
  140
senior managers, training 4–5
Sennett, Richard 11
sex discrimination 6–7
  football 52
  salaries 40
  see also women
shareholders
  directors' pay 34, 36, 37
  power 42–3
  role 86
  value 37
Sharples, Sir James 56
single loop learning 124
skill deficiencies 14–15
slaves
  Greek 76–7
  Roman 82–3

small businesses 20
  case study 21–2
social classes, Egyptians 69–70
social responsibility 31
social science 107–9, 110
solutions 64
South Korea
  economic restructuring 46–7
  financial crisis 44–6
  IMF rescue 45–6
Spangler, David xiii
spiritual gap, Greek civilization
  79–80
statistics, influence of 38
Stewart, Thomas 126
stock exchanges 86
structure 97–8, 113–20, 140–1
  circular 101, 110, 116–17,
    119–20, 136, 147
  matrix 115, 116
  see also network structure
style 6–7
sustainability 105
symbiosis 104
synergy 130
  chain process 131, 141–2
systems thinking 97–8, 100, 110

tactile organization 17–18
talent, management 25–6
Tavistock Clinic 107
teaching 7–8
teams 128
  development 141–2, 144
  learning 121
technology
  growth of 98, 107
  ignorance 18–19
Thailand, financial crisis 43–4
Thatcher, Margaret 30, 31
thermodynamics, second law of 100,
  110, 151

training
  effectiveness 1–3
  examples 3
  management 59–61
  public sector 4–5
transformation viii, 12–13, 62,
    135–41, 149–50
  dialogue 137–8
  involvement 138–41
  resistance to 130–3
Trist, Eric 107
trust 9, 10, 127, 141
  profit v 29–30

UK
  downsizing 16
  ethics committee 49–50
  insider trading 31
  pensions mis-selling 29–30
  productivity 14–15
  scenarios 23
university courses 1
USA, police corruption 57

vision 137–8, 141, 143
von Bertalanffy, Ludwig 97, 107

web structure 96, 118–20
Wells, H. G. 65–6, 149, 153

Wheatley, Margaret 140
whole system approach
    138–9
wholescale technology 139–40
Wired World scenario 23
wisdom 96, 122
women
  ancient Greece 77–8
  Egypt, independence
    70–2
  electorate 40–1
  entrepreneurs 23
  glass ceiling 21
  government 41
  leadership style 6–7
  position 119
  Roman civilization 81
  Russia 47–8
  salaries 40
  self-employment 21
  web structure 119
work
  ancient Egypt 72
  ancient Greece 78
  Roman civilization 81–2
world view 108–9

Zukav, Gary 129

In Search of Leaders
Hilarie Owen
ISBN 0-471-49197-7
Price £17.99

If you enjoyed this book, try *In Search of Leaders*, the prequel to *Unleashing Leaders* in which leadership guru Hilarie Owen builds the foundations for discovering your own potential as a leader. In this thoroughly readable book, traditional views of leadership are blown away as Hilarie demonstrates that leadership is not just for those who have achieved positions at the top of their organization. There is leadership potential in everyone. The question is, how do you release that untapped reservoir of potential? Or, more accurately, how do you transform the reluctant individuals who do not believe they have the raw material to be leaders within their chosen environment? *In Search of Leaders* provides the answers and sets readers firmly on the road to personal responsibility and achievement. Hilarie provides all the motivation and tools you need to unlock your potential and fulfil your own leadership aspirations.

Illustrates brilliantly the importance of understanding the human essence of leadership
Warren Bennis, Distinguished Professor of Business Administration, University of Southern California and Visiting Professor of Leadership, University of Exeter.